Concepts and Theories in
Sociology of Education

THE PROFESSIONAL EDUCATION SERIES

Walter K. Beggs, *Editor*
Dean Emeritus
Teachers College
University of Nebraska

Royce H. Knapp, *Research Editor*
Regents Professor of Education
Teachers College
University of Nebraska

Concepts and Theories in Sociology of Education

by

KEITH W. PRICHARD

Professor
Sociology of Education
University of Nebraska

and

THOMAS H. BUXTON

Assistant Professor
Social Foundations of Education
University of South Carolina

PROFESSIONAL EDUCATORS PUBLICATIONS, INC.
LINCOLN, NEBRASKA

Library of Congress Catalog Card No.: 73-78009

ISBN   0-88224-010-2

© Copyright 1973
by
Professional Educators Publications, Inc.

Contents

Preface

A continuous dialog has been waged for years among sociologists studying the field of education and educational practitioners concerning the nature of sociology of education. Sociologists, on the one hand, have deplored publishing, in the name of sociology of education, philosophical writing of an essay nature lacking empirical data.

On the other hand, educational administrators representing both administrative and teaching personnel describe much of the writing on educational institutions and processes produced by sociologists as having the impact of a limp feather on the practical operational aspects of the school. They maintain that such writing, while of interest to sociological theorists, is often devoid of relevance for the practical day-to-day operation of the schools. Some of the allegations of each camp are justified.

The present volume is intended as a supplementary text in the sociology of education at the beginner level. The authors have endeavored to relate, in as direct a manner as possible, the practical implications of certain sociological theories and concepts to the analysis of educational structures and processes.

In preparation for this volume, the authors conducted a study among a large number of American sociologists to determine the ten individuals who they thought had made the greatest contributions to the field of sociology of education. Heavy emphasis has been placed in this volume on the work of these foremost men and women in this academic specialization. Such individuals include Willard Waller, Wilbur Brookover, Charles Bidwell, James Coleman, Burton Clark, Neal Gross, Harold Hodgkinson, Donald Hansen, C. Wayne Gordon, and Lloyd and Elaine Cook.

The authors have also drawn heavily upon the theories of those men and women in sociology proper. These include Talcott Parsons, Robert K. Merton, Lloyd Warner, Richard Centers, Florence Kluckhohn, Alex Inkeles, and George Spindler.

Finally, it should be noted that the material contained in this volume has been taught with success at several major universities. It is the hope of the authors that its contents have been presented in such a manner as to maximize their application for improving educational structures and processes.

CHAPTER 1

The History and Development of Sociology of Education

What Is Sociology of Education?

Many attempts have been made by sociologists and educators to formulate an adequate definition of sociology of education. Such definitions have varied greatly over the years and have usually met with rejection by either the professionals working in sociology or in education, or by both. Some of the difficulty in securing agreement as to a working definition of sociology of education possibly arises from the marginality of the subject area itself. Sociology of education has on occasion been claimed by sociology and by education as a part of the exclusive domain of each; however, just as often, it has been rejected by both. It has frequently been regarded as an illegitimate child in the world of academia. Second, the promoters of educational psychology and educational philosophy waged vigorous campaigns to convince the public that their subject areas were of great importance in teacher training. The failure of the promoters of sociology of education to "push" their subject area with equal vigor made it appear that this area of academic specialization had comparatively little to offer. As a result, it was given but slight attention by a majority of those responsible for designing and carrying out training programs for professional educators. Third, serious errors made by many of the early workers in sociology of education in not placing sufficient emphasis upon the need for scientific research in the subject area has, until quite recently, left it with a lack of subject matter and, therefore, in a somewhat anemic condition.[1]

Presently, sociology of education is considered a sub-area of sociology, and hence a definition of the larger area may be an essential first step in formulating a working definition of sociology of education itself. Sociology is the scientific study of human society. Sociology concerns itself with the application of scientific methods and techniques to achieve knowledge of the manner in which group life operates within human society. Again, it must be noted that sociology emphasizes the group within society. Unlike psychology, which views human behavior in terms of the individual, sociology concerns itself with analyzing the structure and functioning of groups. More precisely, sociologists examine the origins, composition, and interrelationship of groups as these factors relate to and involve human behavior. In this effort, the sociologists must often go somewhat far afield and examine the environmental, biological, and psychological factors that relate to the group's structure and function.

As a specialized subject within the general area of sociology, sociology of education is chiefly concerned with applying the knowledge, techniques, and methods achieved in sociological study to the group relationships within educational systems and processes. In some instances, the resultant knowledge or skills may lead to the application of solutions to educational problems; however, it is not mandatory that problem solving of an immediate nature be accomplished. Sociology of education may, on occasion, simply serve the purpose of scientific inquiry by revealing the nature of certain relationships among groups or within a group with no immediate applicable findings.

Defining the Principles of Sociology of Education

Before delineating the specific characteristics of sociology of education, it is perhaps necessary to note that teaching methods and subject content of sociology vary widely. All men and women who teach in the subject area must, to a degree, rely heavily upon the concepts and theories they have been taught as undergraduate and graduate students. Certainly this is true for beginning faculty members. Even later, faculty members may be limited in their teaching situations by the types of resources available to them in a given community. Complaints are frequently voiced of the lack of materials available for teaching beginning courses in sociology of education.[2] The present work constitutes an effort on the part of the writers to provide teachers with a working knowledge of the subject area. Sociology of education as an academic subject area confines itself to, and is characterized by, the following delineations:

1. The first principle governing the study of sociology of education is that knowledge obtained in the area be gained by scientific methodology. Sociology of education is concerned with the search for accuracy. In this effort, objective methods are employed. It is basically a science and attempts to achieve a body of empirically testable knowledge. In addition, sociology of education is concerned with systematic theories and techniques of human relationships (group behavior) as they can be applied to educational structures and processes to produce better learning situations for society. In this context, one may wish to investigate the education progress in the public school systems of a group of black children from the urban slums whose families have recently immigrated from the rural South as compared with an equal number of white children from wealthy, suburban homes in communities such as Shaker Heights, Evanston, or Westchester. Scientific objectivity, however, must be clearly sought in obtaining results from such an investigation. Anything less than the best scientific methodology is worthless. Even after the results of the study or investigation have been reported, the good sociologists of education are likely to examine and reexamine the evidence for bias or other prejudicial elements.

2. The knowledge or skills obtained or taught must focus on the educative processes in society. Sociology of education is concerned with education in the broadest sense of the term. It does not deal exclusively with schooling. The concept dealt with is much broader, inclusive of schooling, but also involves lifelong acculturation. The educational situations studied may be relatively informal, unstructured, and attached to no formal institution, as exemplified by a teenage rap session that may take place in a student's home or at the local drugstore. However, some situations studied may be highly formal, structured, and highly institutionalized, such as the teaching that takes place within a classroom of a public school system conducted by a teacher certified by properly authorized officials within the state government. Typically, courses or research in sociology of education focus on such topics as (a) the community and the school, (b) the role of teachers in the community, (c) social class membership and academic success, (d) cultural values and student involvement, or (e) structure of teenage peer groups in schools.

3. The third principle delineating sociology of education is the type of population units considered appropriate for study. By population units we mean the child, the student, the family, the teachers, the principals, the superintendents, school board members, community citizens, etc. Each of these represents a population unit or group that may in one manner or another affect the educative processes and systems, and in turn act to change, modify, or perpetuate much of the present educative system in society. Generalists prefer to focus on a broad spectrum of groups for study and investigation, whereas specialists concentrate on only one or two such population units or groups. In most instances, courses on the undergraduate level tend to emphasize a generalistic approach, while those on the more advanced graduate level frequently deal with relatively few

groups or population units and their relationship to the educative structure and function.

4. The fourth factor delineating sociology of education is that some form of social relationship between the various population units or groups is studied. For example, a survey of recently published articles in sociology of education journals indicates that the following types of relationships are considered worthy of investigation: "Power and Autonomy in Teacher Socialization," "Determinants of Faculty Support for Student Demonstrations," "Role Conflict and Consensus During an Academic Role Transition," "Professional Status and Faculty Support of Student Demonstrations," "Role Conflict and Consensus of Public School Principals," "The Impact of Peer Interaction During an Academic Role Transition," "The Unionization of Teachers: Determinants of Rank-and-File Support," and "Role Model Identity of 142 'Teachers of the Year.'" The type of relationship to be studied is derived largely from the theoretical framework developed by sociology. Thus, it is within the purview of sociology of education to study relationships between cultures, social classes, and role occupiers as they are involved in and related to educational structure and function.

The above principles govern the concepts used in research and the teaching of sociology of education. Priority given to each principle will vary from one faculty member to another, as will the degree of emphasis placed upon each; however, these principles are the basic elements essential to teaching and research work in this academic field. The reader will observe that the writers have not indicated that the research or teaching in sociology of education necessarily leads to or presents material directly applicable to solutions of educational problems. However, the question has frequently been raised in historical dispute as to whether the field should focus upon current problems in education in such a manner as to produce solutions. The aims and goals of sociology of education have long been in dispute, and several schools of thought have developed in support of particular goals and aims during the somewhat turbulent history of the area.

How Did Sociology of Education Develop?

A knowledge of the development of sociology of education in the historical sense is essential for an adequate understanding of many problems that presently confront the field of study, and such knowledge can serve as a basis for understanding the concepts that have been developed within the subject. It should be pointed out in an attempt to trace historical trends, that few areas of knowledge have ever had their followers and practitioners so badly split concerning the goals which the area should seek to develop as has sociology of education. The subject area was developed relatively late, and it has often held the position of an unwanted stepsister.

Almost all sources are in agreement on one thing and that is that sociology of education made its first appearance in Lester Ward's *Dynamic Sociology,* published in 1883. In his last chapter Ward indicated the importance of education as a factor in transforming society.[3] John Dewey added strength to the field when he published *The School and Society* in 1899.[4] It appears that, although a great amount of material was being published during this early period, much of it had little relevance for education. The material was based on unscientific evidence; most writings could be classified as moral philosophy. Many felt they could write and research in the subject area, but few had the ability or training to do so. There were exceptions: Emile Durkheim, William James, and C. S. Peirce, along with Dewey, are often quoted as making significant contributions to the academic area.[5] Durkheim's work is especially important, and perhaps upon him, if any man, can be laid the title of founder of sociology of education; however, some claim the honor for George S. Payne. Durkheim was born in 1858 from a family of rabbinical scholars. He taught secondary school until 1887. After teaching social studies and pedagogy at the University of Bordeau, he was called to the University of Paris. By 1913 he pursuaded the university to accept sociology as a separate academic subject. He was primarily concerned that good scientific methodology be used in the study of education. He was interested in the process of social disintegration in France and suggested that the schools could stem this tide. He viewed the schools as increasingly being forced to acquire the tasks of socializing the child.[6] "Thus, the school possesses everything it needs to awaken in the child the feelings of solidarity, of group life."[7] Although Durkheim had taught in the secondary schools, he was most interested in giving elementary teachers ideas that could be used in classroom situations.[8]

The growth and popularity of the subject in the United States was evidenced by the fact that, while the course had first been introduced in 1907 by Henry Suzzallo, by 1914 as many as 16 institutions were offering courses called educational sociology.[9] Both New York University and Columbia University early recognized the need for sociology of education and presented their students with strong offerings in the academic area. Columbia's Teachers College founded a department of educational sociology in 1916 under the chairmanship of Dr. David Snedden. [10] By the 1920s, 194 colleges and universities in the United States were offering courses in the subject area.[11] The organization of the National Society for the Study of Educational Sociology was begun in the early 1920s under the sponsorship of E. George Payne. [12] Between 1923 and 1931, three yearbooks were issued by the National Society.[13] While sociologists and educational specialists met together, storm warnings began to appear in the late 1920s. There was violent controversy concerning which direction the subject area should take and the order of priorities in its future growth.

The evidence suggests that it was in Germany in the 1920s and 1930s that precise work was being done on which much of the future growth of the subject would depend. Max Weber is usually cited as being extremely important in the development of many concepts later used in sociology of education.[14] He was born in Erfurt, Germany, in 1864. He taught at Berlin, Göttingen, and Heidelberg. The scope and importance of his work was not fully appreciated until after his death. Weber possessed an encyclopedic intellect and thrived in masses of detail. He attempted to analyze education in the context of an industrial-technological society.[15] In this context, Weber saw formal education as a "differentiating agency" in which individuals were prepared for a particular life-style.[16] He suggested that in the future most educational institutions would produce highly trained specialists for the society.[17] Floud and Halsey have noted in their analysis of Weber's contributions to sociological inquiry in education that he viewed education as primarily functioning to prepare each individual for the status in the social structure that he was later to occupy.[18] He saw education as preparing individuals and groups for a particular life-style.[19] Weber had a profound effect upon much of the later research conducted in sociology of education, and his attention to the concept of bureaucracy and social stratification was to dominate much of the research and literature produced in the academic area for the next three decades. The work of Vierkandt and Von Wiese also placed heavy emphasis on the relationship of educational structure to social structure.[20]

With the rise of Hitler to power in Germany in the early 1930s, the development of sociology of education shifted to the American scene. Other European countries were slow to accept the subject area into their college and university curricula. Thus, sociology of education became virtually a monopoly of the United States academic institutions. This period witnessed the entry into the field of many persons trained in sociology. Among the significant contributors were Willard Waller, Wilbur Brookover, Kimball Young, Margaret Mead, Lloyd Warner, Pitirim Sorokin, Florence Greenhoe, Florian Znaniecki, O. C. Smucker, and Elaine and Lloyd Cook. These men and women and others began in one sense a systematic application of concepts of sociology and social psychology to the social phenomena of school life. There is general consensus that Willard Waller, to a greater extent than anyone else, began to point the direction for sociology of education in its future development. In *Sociology of Teaching*, Waller represented the "first major attempt to analyze the role of teachers in relation both to their students and to the communities in which they teach."[21] He dealt heavily with role conflict in the school between teachers and students. He viewed teachers as playing an important part in the process of cultural diffusion. He especially stressed the function of the school in creating conditions of social mobility for large elements of the population. He saw the school as functioning to create a more viable society. He is responsible for applying the concept of social and cultural lag to the analysis of educational problems. "Sociologists have found that many of the unadjustments in modern society are traceable to what is known as cultural lag, to the fact that non-material, or adaptive culture, does not change so rapidly as material culture. Thus our systems of law, religion, and morals are authentic antiques, but our automobiles and radios and talking pictures are modern. Much of the maladjustment of society is due to this failure of the machinery of social control to change with a rapidity equalling that of mechanical culture."[22] Waller's work is still considered to be of great importance; his reputation as a scientific developer of sociology of education is very much intact.

While noteworthy work was being produced in this period, problems of a very serious nature were beginning to arise, which would result in the neglect and near destruction of sociology of education. In fact, the subject area almost disappeared as a valid and reputable academic area by the late 1940s. One of the contributing factors for the near demise of sociology of education was the appearance of another education subject area, educational psychology. Many school administrators felt more at home with this subject and encouraged its growth over that of sociology of education. The administrators appeared to see educational psychology as more practical and less dangerous in its potential than sociology of education. Such practitioners preferred dealing with the individual child in tests and measurements to dealing with the various societal groups in the community and the problems likely to arise from such attempts.

A second factor responsible for the decreasing interest in sociology of education was that many people involved in developing the area were untrained in research. There was a lack of application of adequate research techniques and methods in the work. Much of it was a hodgepodge of material turned out under the title of educational sociology.[23] Further, many untrained faculty were teaching in the academic area. Herrington noted a reduction in the number of courses offered from 1926 to 1947.[24] Brookover, writing in 1949, noted that much of the curricula taught under the title of educational sociology was composed of material much of which had little or nothing to do with education or sociology.[25] He noted that by the late 1940s, departments and schools of education appeared to prefer sending their students straight to courses in sociology rather than dealing with the hodgepodge.[26] With the exceptions of New York University, where a strong and diversified set of offerings was given in sociology of education, and Wayne University in Detroit, where a very strong department had been founded in the early 1940s, the field appeared to be in a very definite period of retraction or eminent collapse.

The chief reason for the loss of interest in the development of sociology of education was apparently that the practitioners and theoreticians in the area were completely split regarding the direction the field should take, and controversy raged as to how to best develop the area. Clearly two very different orientations had begun to develop with several subdivisions characteristic of each. With the recently developed work done in the United States in establishing publishing journals and public relations agencies, such controversy was easily aired. The journals of the period contained "heated" letters to the editors espousing one view or another.

One school of thought tended to view the subject area as a branch of sociology and applied the term of sociology of education to the field. Another group, however, composed of school administrators, educational specialists, and professors of education, tended to view the field as properly belonging to education. This latter group was primarily concerned with the direct application of sociological theory to school problems. They sought to balance the influence of educational psychology and educational philosophy by including the study of sociology in education. This school of thought tended to label the subject as educational sociology.

Brookover noted in 1949 that as many as half a dozen different minor schools of thought were flourishing in the field, thus adding confusion to an already chaotic situation.[27] Table I[28] indicates the general nature of the fragmentation that was occurring at this time in the academic area. The categorization is based largely upon Brookover's early analysis.

A final problem in this area has been revealed by Donald A. Hansen in "The Uncomfortable Relation of Sociology and Education," in which he suggests that sociology itself as the newest of the social sciences was under pressure at this time to prove its own legitimacy.[29] It can only be surmised that the professional workers in sociology would look with great misgivings and mistrust upon a newly emerging subject such as sociology of education or educational sociology and thus be inclined to regard it as somewhat an ugly duckling. Just as the sociologists themselves were beginning to achieve respectability, a less tested and less legitimate issue appeared and reflected badly on its parentage, sociology proper.[30] That sociologists tended to sabotage the development of sociology of education or educational sociology may be suspected but cannot be proved. It is probable that sociologists recognized the difficulties being encountered by educational sociology and the embarrassment resulting to the parent, sociology, and therefore moved in and attempted to direct the future of this subject area. However, those who perceived the role of the subject in terms of the goals generally set forth by educational sociologists were not completely happy with this trend. Letters to the editors of the national publications in the field reflect the conflict of the period.

Indicative of the conflict of opinion over the direction the subject area should take is the method of titling books of the period that has continued to a certain extent into the present period. Few textbook writers dared to directly tie both sociology and education together in a manner that might antagonize some particular point of view. Instead, textbooks were apt to skirt the issue by using titles such as *A Sociological Approach to Education*,[31] *Education and Society*,[32] or *Education and Social Order*.[33] Nonetheless, with the entry into the field of many trained sociologists such as Neal Gross, Charles Bidwell, Robert Havighurst, and others, the subject field began to move toward a sociological school of thought, and the social pattern orientation as indicated in Table I

TABLE I

General Divisions and Definitions	Sub-Branches or Minor Schools and Definitions
	(a) **Social Work Orientation** Viewed education as a means of social progress by which school could serve as an agency of change by which people would voice their views and determine future of society.
(1) **Educational Sociology** Saw area as properly belonging in education. Desired a balance for educational psychology and educational philosophy. Wanted useful and practical solutions to educational problems.	(b) **Technical Training Orientation** Saw sociology as a system of tools by which the professionals in the area could teach certain techniques for better dealing with school problems to each teacher and administrator.
	(c) **Philosophic Orientation** Concerned primarily with attempting to formulate a philosophy through which society itself could be analyzed and needs of people could be reflected in curriculum and goals for school.
	(a) **World Orientation** Considered whole process of socialization as their domain. Extended the field of interest from anthropology to psychology.
(2) **Sociology of Education** Viewed subject as properly part of sociology. Defined function as achievement of theoretical knowledge by means of disciplined scientific methods.	(b) **Research Orientation** Concerned with training educational workers and administrators for educational research that largely centered on sociology. Emphasized need to provide teachers, research workers, and others in education with adequate training in sociological methods and techniques.
	(c) **Social Patterns Orientation** Emphasized patterns of social interaction and social roles within society and relationship of these within school and to outside groups.

began to dominate the field. Concern with patterns of roles, values, and social stratification, as they related to schools and educational systems, proved to be the wave of the future in the subject field.

The demise of the National Society for the Study of Educational Sociology came about in the late 1930s. Up to that time, both sociologists and educational specialists had met together. However, their interests and orientations were too incongruent. While the sociologists and those sympathizing with that general orientation had gradually established their control of the subject field, official notification of this fact did not occur until 1963, when the official publication, *Journal of Educational Sociology*,[34] was renamed *Sociology of Education* and placed under the control of a new and different group of people. The new editorial staff and board were represented by men and women largely trained in sociology, with major interests in education. The journal tended to place heavy emphasis upon articles containing statistical data and scientific methodology, whereas earlier articles in *Journal of Educational Sociology* had dealt with morality, policy, and ideas capable of direct educational application.

The Present Status of Sociology of Education

With the entry of large numbers of trained sociologists into the field of sociology of education in the 1950s and 1960s, it was felt that the subject area would begin to develop into a vital and essential part of academia. It appeared that the sociologists had better means of publicizing the subject than had formerly been available to the educational specialists. The American Sociological Association created a special section for sociologists of education within its structure in an effort to stimulate interest in the area. Several prestigious colleges and universities began to have a new look at the academic area. The School of Education at Harvard University developed a small, but interesting, graduate-level program in sociology of education that attempted to combine sociology, education, statistics, and social psychology in a meaningful and practical manner. The program was organized chiefly by Neal Gross, who was concerned with applying sociological theory and technique to an analysis of the role behavior of public school personnel. A synthesis of courses, including academic areas related to sociology and education, was seen as a means of eliminating the schizoid condition that had so long plagued the subject area.

Further impetus for growth and development in sociology of education undoubtedly was provided by federal legislative and executive acts that attempted to produce equal educational and occupational opportunity for minority and low income groups. During the presidency of Lyndon B. Johnson, attention to the socially disadvantaged produced a great interest and consequent growth in sociology of education in institutions of higher learning. In the late 1950s only a few dozen colleges and universities offered courses in sociology of education or educational sociology; by the late 1960s, over 150 such institutions were listing courses in sociology of education or educational sociology. Thus, at least in terms of quantitative measures, as reflected in the number of schools offering courses in the area, sociology of education or educational sociology was almost back to its level in the late 1920s, when approximately 200 institutions provided offerings in the area.

Nonetheless, the argument over the true nature, aims, and goals of the subject area did not cease. Because of the dominance of sociologists in sociology of education, several professionals have continued to argue for the production of research and information that is of immediate and practical use to educators rather than the largely theoretical material currently being produced by sociologists of education. Gale E. Jensen views the material currently being produced as having little relevance for education.[35] He voices the need for separating the subject area into sociology of education and educational sociology, with the latter subject concentrating on immediate solutions to educational problems and approaching such problems from the point of interest of educators rather than that of sociologists.[36] He appears to view sociology of education and educational sociology in much the same relationship as architecture holds to engineering, with the latter in each case being chiefly interested in and concerned with solving problems of an immediate and relevant nature.[37] Several British authors have also advocated a separation of the two areas. Taylor, writing in *The Study of Education*, has suggested that the separate use of the two terms, sociology of education and educational sociology, be maintained in order to preserve the distinction between an emphasis on educational problems and an emphasis on sociological problems.[38]

There currently appears to be an underlying fear that the academic area, and particularly that labeling itself as sociology of education, is coming under the complete dominance of sociologists. Even Hansen in his analysis of "the uncomfortable relationship between sociology and education" has suggested that, while the problem frequently faced is the wide separation of the sociologists and educators, it might possibly be even more disastrous should sociology of education come under the total and complete dominance of sociology and be unable to maintain and develop its separate interests.[39] A great many professionals, especially the educational specialists, tend to fear that this has already happened.

To the contrary, most practitioners in the subject field have tended to view the field as closely interrelated and not capable of separation; sociology of education and educational sociology are the same for all practical purposes, and both are closely tied to sociology itself. E. B. Reuter, as quoted by Brookover and Gottlieb, indicates that "the interests of the educational sociologist differ from those of the general sociologist only in the fact that he works with a specially selected set of materials. . . . He is interested in understanding the behavior and ideologies of school men, in discovering the effects of school on existing institutions and its influence on personality."[40]

In short, the problem appears capable of being prolonged for a considerable time. In an attempt to answer the complaints of those primarily concerned with application of solutions to educational problems, Charles Bidwell, editor-in-chief of *Sociology of Education* has designed a section in the national organ entitled "Research Notes," in which the more applicable materials are included. In other attempts to synthesize the basic differences into a meaningful unity, Orville Brim, well known for his work in sociology of education and in sociology, has suggested that joint appointments be given to faculty members in departments of sociology and in schools of education as a method of resolving the dilemma.[41] It is generally conceded by most authorities that it would behoove men and women who prepare for careers in teaching or research in sociology of education to combine in one manner or another curricula from both education and sociology. Authoritative opinion generally urges a form of hybridization in such a manner that the candidate first obtains an A.B. degree in the broad liberal arts area with some specialization in sociology.[42] Should the candidate for the position have obtained a master's degree in education and worked to a considerable extent within elementary or secondary schools, he would be well advised to take his doctoral work within the sociology department. To the contrary, should the candidate be heavily backgrounded in sociology and have very limited experience in education and the school systems, it is usually felt that he should take his doctoral work in the school of education.

In order to gauge the extent to which sociology of education or educational sociology is presently taught in the institutions of higher learning in the United States, the writers contacted the academic deans or provosts at 500 major academic institutions of higher learning in the United States in the fall of 1972.[43] Data from the findings indicate that sociology of education or educational sociology is taught by 257 men and women at 199 institutions. The University of Chicago appears to maintain the single largest faculty in this area of academic specialization. The data suggest further that the greatest growth in the development of courses in sociology of education or educational sociology is taking place among the newly organized branches of the major state universities. Such new branches of the state universities are often located in

large urban areas previously unserved by universities, and many such
institutions appear to recognize the value of offerings in sociology of
education or educational sociology for students and residents in their
immediate area.

The evidence further suggests that during the five-year period from
1967 to 1972 the 199 institutions offering courses in the academic area
of specialization have produced 173 doctorates and 285 master's degrees
in either sociology of education or educational sociology. The twelve
schools listed in Table II lead in the production of graduate degrees
in this area for the stated time period.

TABLE II

TWELVE INSTITUTIONS OF HIGHER LEARNING PRODUCING LARGEST NUMBER OF
GRADUATE DEGREES IN SOCIOLOGY OF EDUCATION OR
EDUCATIONAL SOCIOLOGY

School	Number of Doctorates	Number of Master's
1. Wayne State University	21	82
2. Harvard University	19	0
3. New York University	10	40
4. U.C.L.A.	10	25
5. Michigan State University	10	5
6. University of Southern California	10	0
7. Stanford University	9	10
8. University of California	6	1
9. Rutgers Graduate School of Education	5	20
10. Purdue University	5	12
11. Fordham University	2	4
12. California State College at L.A.	0	16

The data collected also suggest that there continues to be a lack of
consensus as to whether sociology of education and educational
sociology should be properly tied together under the same title
or whether they are separate and distinct areas of academia. Table III
gives some indication of the continuing division in the general area. It
will be noted that generally departments of sociology tend to associate
themselves with the title of sociology of education, whereas schools of
education are more apt to associate themselves with the title of educational sociology.

Analysis of research findings with respect to popularity of texts in
sociology of education or educational sociology reveals a wide variety
of choices. In a study done in 1961 Hoyme found there was much confusion or diversity in the use of texts.[44] Forty-nine different textbooks

TABLE III

RELATIONSHIP OF TITLE OF ACADEMIC AREA TO
SCHOOLS AND DEPARTMENTS

Title of Course(s)	Offered in Department(s) of Education	Offered in Sociology Department(s)
Educational Sociology	109	33
Sociology of Education	45	128

were used by 168 professors. The three most used in order of frequency were (1) Havighurst and Neugarten, *Society and Education;* (2) Smith, Stanley, Benne, and Anderson, *Social Foundations of Education;* and (3) Brookover, *A Sociology of Education.*[45] Snyder, in a study done in 1968, noted that the most frequently cited texts and supplementary readings used in undergraduate courses in sociology of education were (1) Ronald Corwin, *A Sociology of Education;* (2) Halsey, Floud, and Anderson, *Education, Economy, and Society;* (3) Brookover and Gottlieb, *A Sociology of Education;* and (4) Clark, *Educating the Expert Society.*[46] In the same study Snyder found that three texts received equally high citations by the faculty members teaching on the graduate level in the subject area. These were Clark, *Educating the Expert Society;* Corwin, *A Sociology of Education;* and Halsey, Floud, and Anderson, *Education, Economy, and Society.*[47] Many of the faculty members who replied to Hoyme's questionnaire noted that no textbook was precisely designed for a course of study in sociology of education because (1) the academic preparation of instructors would direct the subject matter and such preparation was very different from each other; (2) the objective varied widely, necessitating different approaches and texts; and (3) the quality of the students varied greatly, and this dictated the uses of the texts.[48] The above additional comments on the questionnaires reveal the problems confronting faculty members in the subject area and suggest a continuation of many of the earlier problems dealt with in the historical review.

The foregoing historical evidence and review of the present status of sociology of education suggest that the field has clearly not made the progress that might have been hoped for by the founders who worked in the area some 70 or more years ago. Today, undergraduate courses in the academic field are relatively rare. While a few hundred doctoral candidates have been produced by the major institutions of higher learning in the past few years, these figures scarcely bear comparison to the several thousands who have been graduated with doctorates in educational psychology, educational philosophy, and history of education. Certainly, the relative productivity of sociology of education cannot be related to lack of interest on the part of the public schools or to low levels of demand on the part of urban areas or governmental programs, for these areas have urged qualified sociologists of education to work with them. Undoubtedly a vacuum has been created by the failure of sociologists of education to provide sufficient numbers of individuals with the needed training to enter the various fields involving social knowledge and educational processes.

Reasons Educators Should Study Sociology of Education

Having read the foregoing historical review of the development of sociology of education and analyzed the present status of the academic area, one may ask why sociology of education should be studied. Following is a list of some of the important reasons why this subject area should be included in the academic background of educators, and why it is essential for workers, teachers, and researchers concerned with the behavorial sciences and educational processes to have a working knowledge of sociology of education.

1. Educators today more than ever before must have the conceptual tools and social skills to teach students from families of various social classes, of various races, national origins, and from very different types of neighborhood environments. In a period of increasing integration of students within the same buildings and same classrooms, educators need to understand the meaning of these basic social differences in terms of the effects they have upon the student's style of learning, the student's perception of his life chances, and the student's social mobility. Sociology of education helps to convey this knowledge.

2. Sociology of education can provide the teacher with a more complete view of the school, the community, and the student than can be realized alone by a study of educational psychology, educational philosophy, and educational history. Sociology of education gives the educator a degree of balance in knowledge of human behavior that would otherwise not be obtainable.

3. The educator today is confronted with a need to interpret research articles, to do basic statistical studies, and in general, to achieve a certain level of competence in research in order to better deal with the modern teaching situation. Sociology of education is one of the prime subject areas through which scientific knowledge and research methods and techniques in dealing with group behavior can be achieved.

4. A study of sociology of education helps the educator avoid provincialism in his professional behavior and attitudes, since a concern and interest in sociology of education broadens the experience and hence the tolerance of educators. In short, the subject provides the educator with knowledge of the merits of others' cultures. He may be better equipped as a result of studying sociology of education to serve as a teacher in a different culture or in a geographic area very different from that of his own childhood socialization.

5. Those educators responsible for policy making can gain considerable knowledge of the social forces that influence education and the ways in which the educational system is affected by them through studying sociology of education. A knowledge of the particular attitudes and behaviors of certain population elements within the community can help to smooth the way for social changes being introduced into the society via the school system.

6. All educators can gain from a study of sociology of education a better view of the different roles that are performed within the school itself. A knowledge of the fact that groups of teachers hold for themselves and for their colleagues different role expectations than may be held by other groups should help all educators to more effectively operate within the same institutional structures. Two school administrators may operate in the same position in very different manners, owing to the fact that they hold quite different sets of role expectations as to what the job requires. One may view the job as basically working with minority students in providing opportunities for their upward social mobility. Another administrator may view the essential part of the job as being to provide well rounded curricula for all students or to educate a scientific elite. A study of sociology of education can provide educators with a knowledge of the different role interpretations and hence a greater tolerance for others' role definitions.

7. Sociology of education can make substantial contributions, along with educational psychology and educational philosophy, by helping educators to determine policies that will work among certain population units and those that will not. In policy making, sociology of education can be used to help determine the aims or objectives which the school and the community should seek to achieve. This subject area can be used to help determine the social behavior sought as a result of school programs. While educational psychology may help to determine individual learning performance, sociology of education can be used to determine group behavioral goals to be included in any educational program.

What Concepts Are Studied in Sociology of Education?

As has been noted, the objectives vary greatly from instructor to instructor because of the differences in academic backgrounds and materials available. Nonetheless, the classroom teacher must to the best of his ability spell out and organize the concepts and theories included in the area of academic specialization, in this case, sociology of education. The classroom teacher must usually build his course around a set of general ideas and concepts. If his students are to study sociology of education with understanding, they must possess a knowledge of the basic concepts used in the field. It appears that some method for categorizing the information is necessary. Blumer has noted that concepts are "fundamentally sensitizing instruments."[49] He has noted that "it gives the users a general sense of reference and guidance in approaching empirical instances. . . ."[50]

Just what are concepts? It may generally be said that concepts help the individual working in the behavioral sciences to establish the boundaries and limitations of things to be analyzed. The sociologist of education must always remember that concepts are merely assumptions. They may or may not be true. They are simply the best guesses. There are great advantages to using concepts and Bruner has noted these to be: (1) it reduces the complexity of the environment; (2) it is the means by which the objects of the environment are identified; (3) it reduces the necessity of relearning at each new encounter; (4) it helps provide for direction, prediction, and planning for activity; and (5) it permits ordering and relating classes of objects or phenomena.[51] Every teacher or researcher in sociology of education, in order to be effective in the area, needs to have some understanding of the central concepts of the academic discipline.

In 1968 Snyder undertook to investigate the concepts most frequently used by members of the Sociology of Education Section of the American Sociological Association in their classroom teaching. While there were some differences in the use of concepts depending on the level at which the faculty members were teaching, undergraduate, graduate, or advanced graduate, certain concepts were found to be heavy choices of the practitioners at each level. Concepts heavily relied on in teaching were (1) social stratification and education; (2) social roles and career patterns of teachers; (3) education as an institution; (4) the school as a social system; (5) education of the culturally different and deprived; (6) social structure and organization; and (7) teacher-student roles in education.[52]

In 1961 Hoyme asked sociologists and educational specialists teaching sociology of education to indicate from a list of 64 concepts (1) whether the concept was appropriate and (2) whether the concept was taught in the faculty member's present course. The concepts having highest scores in terms of importance were (1) social status; (2) social mobility; (3) social change and social conflict; (4) social class structure; (5) school and its social implications; (6) social roles; (7) community; (8) American society; (9) classical sociological studies; and (10) school and community relations. The sociologists in the same study indicated a slightly different preference in concepts which they deemed essential to an understanding of sociology of education. Their priority list alone is as follows: (1) social class structure; (2) democracy and education; (3) race relations; (4) social status; (5) social roles; (6) social objectives of education; (7) teacher as social being; (8) teacher-student relations; (9) teacher-administrator relations; and (10) community.[53]

Meltzer and Mannis, reporting in a survey done for UNESCO in "The Teaching of Sociology," entitled *The Teaching of Social Sciences in the United States,* suggest that the concepts most apt to be studied are (1) social stratification and education; (2) social class mobility in relation to educational opportunities; (3) racial segregation and desegregation in schools; (4) ability grouping in schools; (5) classroom social structure; (6) student role expectations and aspirations; (7) status and roles of teachers; (8) educational and social policy; and (9) culture and the schools.[54]

In a study done by the writers in 1973, 257 faculty members were asked to indicate the concepts which they actually used in their classroom teaching. Again, slight differences occurred with respect to whether the faculty member was teaching undergraduate or graduate students; however, certain concepts were indicated as essential in the teaching at all levels. These were (1) social class or stratification; (2) culture and education; (3) the school as a social organization; (4) education and social change; (5) role and function of teachers; (6) social control and education; (7) research methods in the area; (8) community and school; and (9) socialization and education.

Relationship of Sociology of Education to the Behavioral Sciences

The authors have arranged in Table IV the subject areas involving human behavior in the educative process in relationship to each other in such a manner as to indicate as precisely as possible their relative positions to sociology of education. Thus, one notes that educational anthropology encompasses the outermost circle, since it deals with man's educative processes from the period when he first appeared on earth to the present state of his development. Educational anthropology stresses the universals of man in his socialization and acculturation processes. The second ring encompasses sociology of education. Thus, the universals have been broken down to group behavior in relationship to education. Next, the third ring composes those subject areas such as educational psychology, in which the group processes and behaviors are replaced with concern for the individual's learning processes. Finally, the innermost rings contain those subject areas such as clinical psychology or medical studies in which the physiological or innermost man

TABLE IV

RELATIONSHIP OF BEHAVIORAL SCIENCES IN EDUCATION
TO SOCIOLOGY OF EDUCATION

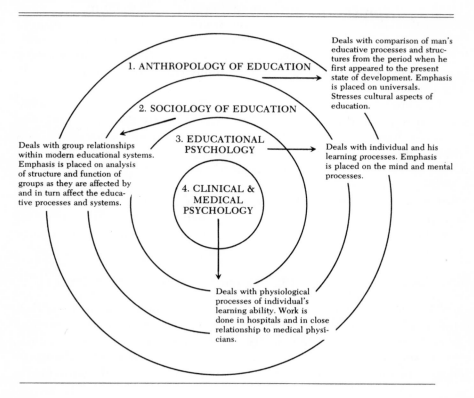

1. ANTHROPOLOGY OF EDUCATION

Deals with comparison of man's educative processes and structures from the period when he first appeared to the present state of development. Emphasis is placed on universals. Stresses cultural aspects of education.

2. SOCIOLOGY OF EDUCATION

Deals with group relationships within modern educational systems. Emphasis is placed on analysis of structure and function of groups as they are affected by and in turn affect the educative processes and systems.

3. EDUCATIONAL PSYCHOLOGY

Deals with individual and his learning processes. Emphasis is placed on the mind and mental processes.

4. CLINICAL & MEDICAL PSYCHOLOGY

Deals with physiological processes of individual's learning ability. Work is done in hospitals and in close relationship to medical physicians.

is studied in relationship to his learning. In this manner, the subjects taught in the behavioral sciences move from the macroscopic to the microscopic, with sociology of education occupying a somewhat middle position. It is not so much concerned with universal mankind or with the individualized man, as with the group behavior of the human species within the educational process.

Just as the subject area of sociology of education appears to lie somewhere between educational anthropology and educational psychology, so the concepts found to be essential to the teaching of sociology of education appear to be capable of gradation, with some concepts lying closer to the broad cultural level of educational anthropology or, to the other extreme, toward the educational psychological field of study.

The present text is organized in such a manner as to present the reader with a knowledge of concepts in sociology of education that move from the macroscopic to the microscopic. Table V reflects an attempt to illustrate the relationship of these concepts to each other. It will be noted that Chapter 2 in the book contains a review of the concepts that are on the outer perimeter and closely related to those that apply also to educational anthropology, such as culture, mores, values, etc. Chapter 3 deals with the concepts contained in the second ring in Table V. These concepts are somewhat more distant from educational anthropology and deal with man's systems of social stratification and social class composition as they relate to educational structures and processes. Chapter 4 contains the concepts of status, social roles, role behavior, role expectations, etc., as they relate to educational personnel. As we draw near the behavioral studies concerning themselves with the individual, such as the various branches of psychology and educational psychology, we find those concepts used in sociology of education that deal with social personality and education. These concepts are contained in Chapter 5.

The arrangement of grading the concepts usually taught by sociologists of education from those of the broadest type, often inclusive of concepts used by the anthropologists, to those of a more individualized nature and sometimes included among the tools of the psychologists, should provide the student or the teacher with a working framework for handling the materials contained in the present manuscript. A review of the concepts found by researchers to be included in teaching the academic area in general fit into one or another of the areas indicated in Table V.

It must be remembered, however, that sociology of education is more or less in a developmental stage, and as one of the newest of the behavioral sciences, its practitioners are not in complete agreement on the concepts that are needed in the teaching of the subject area. Thus, some may well emphasize in their teaching those concepts that are close to and often used by the educational anthropologists; others, with possibly different training and backgrounds, may use the concepts that are closely related to educational psychologists. However, virtually all sociologists of education place heavy emphasis on the concepts contained in the middle rings of Table V; and few, if any, argue

TABLE V

INTRA-RELATIONSHIP OF CONCEPTS INCLUDED IN SOCIOLOGY OF EDUCATION

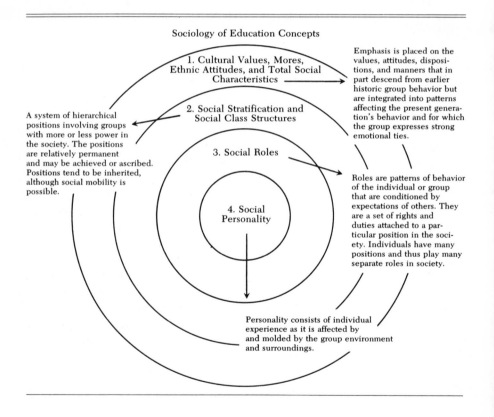

Sociology of Education Concepts

1. Cultural Values, Mores, Ethnic Attitudes, and Total Social Characteristics

2. Social Stratification and Social Class Structures

3. Social Roles

4. Social Personality

Emphasis is placed on the values, attitudes, dispositions, and manners that in part descend from earlier historic group behavior but are integrated into patterns affecting the present generation's behavior and for which the group expresses strong emotional ties.

A system of hierarchical positions involving groups with more or less power in the society. The positions are relatively permanent and may be achieved or ascribed. Positions tend to be inherited, although social mobility is possible.

Roles are patterns of behavior of the individual or group that are conditioned by expectations of others. They are a set of rights and duties attached to a particular position in the society. Individuals have many positions and thus play many separate roles in society.

Personality consists of individual experience as it is affected by and molded by the group environment and surroundings.

the justification of their composing the central base of the subject area.

The gradation of the concepts used in the present work is meant to provide the reader with a better organizational form than is usually presented for studying sociology of education. In moving from the larger or more universal type concepts to the more individualized ones, it is hoped that the reader will achieve an understanding of the concepts that will implement his work with educational theory and practices.

CHAPTER 2

Concepts of Culture and Their Relevance for Education

What Is Culture?

As has been previously noted, some concepts used in sociology of education are macroscopic in nature and are closely related to those used in educational anthropology. They deal with relatively large units of social behavior. Such concepts usually center on the idea of culture. One may define culture in many ways. Generally, one is said to be "cultured" who has a genuine liking for and competence in the arts, literature, and foreign languages. However, this is not the meaning of culture as used by social scientists. Culture refers to that body of knowledge of skills which has been produced by human societies over a long span of time and has been passed on from one generation to the next. Culture consists of all the man-made aspects of the environment. Thus, culture is an all-inclusive phenomenon. It includes man's language, his beliefs, his attitudes, his modern or primitive methods of production, his educational system, and all of his belongings.[1] The concept of culture is wide-ranging and complex. Culture makes up the whole of man's knowledge and skills. Since it is accumulated, each new generation is able to short-circuit much of the learning process and in turn to build up an even greater amount of cultural affluence to pass on to the next generation. Culture not only consists of the artifacts and material type of possessions, but perhaps even more importantly for sociologists of education, culture also includes sets of patterns of behavior and attitudes that are taught by one generation and modified by life experiences of the present generation. Such patterns of attitude and behavior are held to be the right or appropriate patterns on the part of the people who hold them.[2]

It may be said that there is a general national culture for most regions of the world. Thus, we have a general western European culture which has certain characteristics and patterns of thought and behavior that differ significantly from those cultural characteristics of the Orient.[3] There is generally considered to be an American culture as well. The chief exponents or publicizers of this culture to foreign places are undoubtedly the movie industry, the military forces stationed around the world, tourists from the United States, and educational institutions in the United States to which thousands of young foreigners come yearly to earn degrees.

It is recognizable, however, that not everyone holds with equal fervor the same cultural patterns of beliefs and actions throughout the country, but that we have as well smaller groups, called sub-cultures, that vary to a degree in their beliefs and actions from the major groups. For example, Mexican-Americans, Polish-Americans, Chinese-Americans, etc., may hold relatively different attitudes and beliefs from those of the majority groups in the country. Such distinctively different beliefs and habits have been produced as a result of relatively different historic environments of the peoples. Many newly emerging groups (in the political and economic sense) have brought to the American shores cultural patterns of attitude and behavior that vary to a degree from those held by many of the earlier white settlers who arrived from the British Isles, the Low Lands of northern Europe, Germany, and the Scandinavian countries. This latter group have, it is assumed, been subjected to the so-called "melting pot" process and had their cultural patterns mutated and blended to a degree that they are part of the general American culture. This appears not to have taken place to the same degree for blacks and later arriving immigrants.[4]

Great controversy rages today over the extent to which any one of the newer groups or sub-cultures should attempt or be permitted to retain its distinctiveness or its own set of cultural patterns. There appears generally in the past few years in America a tendency to permit greater freedom for sub-cultural groups to develop and to be distinct. Nonetheless, quite often, such separateness has been legally discouraged by governmental laws. For example, certain agriculturally oriented sub-cultural groups may insist that it is their cultural pattern of behavior to permit their children to attend school only until they have completed the eighth grade, at which time they must drop out. However, majority groups of the same geographic region frequently insist that all children must attend school until they have reached the age of sixteen and have passed laws requiring all parents to comply. We usually refer to this type of condition as culture conflict. Increasingly, the American society is troubled by cultural conflict. A recent example of culture conflict is that of the Chinese-American sub-culture in the San Francisco area. Many of the members of the Chinese-American sub-culture wish to preserve and perpetuate the Chinese language and ancestral customs by having them taught in the public schools to the next generation. Cross-bussing policies carried out by city and state officials disrupt this process. The sub-culture as well as the majority groups are thereby placed in a distress situation, culture conflict, as to whether to pursue the general pattern of the major cultural groups or to permit the continued growth of a sub-culture that composes a near majority of the society within that relatively small geographic region. Similarly, in some instances, blacks in the large urban areas across the country have insisted that their sub-cultural patterns of behavior and attitude be permitted to exist and grow, for which purpose they have frequently established private store-front type schools. Situations in which many sub-cultural patterns are permitted to grow and flourish alongside the major ones constitute what is referred to by sociologists and philosophers as a pluralistic society.

Teachers and school administrators, whether they wish it or not, are involved in the cultural question. The curricula they teach, the educational policies they pursue, and the type of structures they institute reflect their solutions to the question of cultural diversity. For educators to proceed without examining the basic sociological issues would indeed be dangerous. Unfortunately, many do just that.

Culture, Core Values, and Education

Some years ago, Ralph Linton, a scholar in sociology and anthropology, suggested that culture may be viewed as an overall plan or design for living.[5] He further noted that culture usually consists of two distinctively different parts. There is a solid core of culture in which, according to Linton, the patterns of behavior and attitudes held are well defined, traditional, and relatively stable.[6] These patterns are held by the major groups within a society. Surrounding this solid core are other more "fluid" patterns in an unintegrated zone around the central core culture.[7] He suggests that the center core contains the values, patterns, and ideas having general acceptance in the society, while the rim patterns, values, and ideas are the "alternatives" or the options which the society permits its groups.[8] His concept is most insightful, and while written in 1936, has relevance for sociologists of education and educators generally. He notes that in times of social upheaval and rapid change, the relationship of one set of patterns, values, and ideas to the other is altered, thus introducing disorder into the society.[9] Pressure is exerted on the core values and patterns, and according to Linton, there tends to be a loss of core values and patterns.[10] He suggests, from the vantage point of the 1930s, that the loss of allegiance to these basic core values and adherence to counter-cultural patterns produces a dangerous situation.[11] Cook and Cook further suggest that as a consequence of this pressure upon the core values and patterns, there tends to be "culture conflict and consequent social disorganization."[12]

Robert C. Angell in *The Integration of American Society* tends to hold views similar to those of Linton and others concerning the core cultural pattern concept, except that in his analysis he uses the group as population unit of study.[13] Harold Hodgkinson may have put it best when he observed that the central core of values operates in something of the manner of a magnet, with the deviant or alternate types of values whirling about the core. The deviant or alternate values attempt to pull the culture apart, whereas the core attempts to pull the whole system together.[14] Such an example has merit in gaining an understanding of the cultural processes taking place in the society.

To put this concept into educational perspective, it may be suggested that teachers and school administrators tend to be relatively conservative in their educational endeavors; that is to say, they conserve the learning which the culture has thus far established. Educators are often thought of as teaching the core cultural patterns of attitude and behavior. As a result, many sub-cultural groups have demonstrated their complete unhappiness with this situation. They insist that their children have suffered from culture conflict in that what is accepted as right and wrong within their own cultural grouping is not the same as that being taught as right and wrong within the formalized instruction of the school systems. They are probably correct to some extent.

Demands for their own neighborhood schools probably reflect this problem.

Most behavioral scientists, in dealing with core cultural patterns and their relationship to the marginal patterns groups within a society, tend to use the concept of cultural values or value orientations in their analyses. The concept of cultural values is one of particular relevance to sociologists of education and to educators as well. It appears to permit analysis of cultures in an efficient manner. In short, each cultural group selects certain conditions of living, certain attitudes toward possessions, certain attitudes toward divinity, etc., as being the most appropriate for that grouping or culture. The Kluckhohns and others, in order to approach the problems of cultural variation, designed a system aimed at the highly generalized components of culture which were labeled as value orientations.[15] In short, they assume that there is a limited number of common human problems for which all people at all times must find solutions. The problems may, they suggest, be capable of variable solutions; however, there are definite limitations on the number of such possible solutions that a given culture may select.[16] The Kluckhohns indicate that certain value orientations selected by the large major groups within a society become the dominant values of that society and that, where different value orientations are selected by other smaller and less important groups, these values become the variant ones within the society.[17] Thus, this concept of culture does not differ significantly from that postulated by Linton.

The importance of the Kluckhohn theory is that it attempts to enumerate and enunciate the particular limited choices of values and value objects presented to groups and societies. The Kluckhohns have outlined the major problems faced by groups and individuals as members of any culture as being: (1) defining their relationship to fellow man—this is the problem of government, or who shall make the decisions; (2) defining their relationship to nature—this is the problem of science; (3) defining how man is born—this is the problem of philosophy, or in some instances, psychology; (4) defining what types of possessions are desirable—this is the problem of capitalism, mercantilism, communism, or economics, etc.; (5) defining to what extent the people within the cultural grouping must work—this is the problem of labor and division of labor; and (6) defining where the people or cultural group exists within the time dimension.[18] In short, the Kluckhohns projected a theory dealing with specifics by which sociologists of education can attempt to describe in a more exact manner just which value orientations are being perpetuated and propagated within the school system and which ones are not.[19] In addition, through such a system of analysis it is possible to more clearly study the variant value orientations of minority groups and those of the lower social class members. The Kluckhohns have presented educators with a specific set of conceptual tools with which to analyze the cultural orientations of the school and its personnel as well as groups within the larger community. These specific orientations are reviewed in depth later in this chapter. We may then examine to what degree educators do tend to perpetuate the values of the core cultural group in Linton's frame of reference and to what degree other non-core cultural groups are being neglected in having their values espoused within the schools.

Talcott Parsons maintains that at present, while the core values within the culture are under attack, they are surviving, and those groups and individuals adhering to the core values have merely shifted in the specific manners in which they project such values.[20] Parsons has developed a set of concepts called pattern variables which define the meaning of given situations and indicate ways of resolving decisional dilemmas. Like the Kluckhohns' theory, this one suggests limited numbers of alternatives. The cultural pattern variables are (1) the basis of choice of the object to which an orientation applies (ascription-achievement); (2) the appropriateness or inappropriateness of immediate gratification through expressive action in the particular context (effectivity-neutrality); (3) the scope of interest in and obligation toward the object (specificity-diffuseness); (4) the type of norm governing the orientation toward it (universalism-particularism); (5) the relevance or irrelevance of collective obligations in the immediate context (self-collective orientation).[21] In many respects, these modes of choice are not markedly different from those postulated by the Kluckhohns.

The thesis projected by Parsons is that the actor or person within the cultural grouping is always confronted by these five choices and that the choices themselves exhaust the logical number of alternatives.[22] Every individual or group, in fact, provides answers to them in every facet of social action in which he engages. Each alternate choice will find in some particular cultural grouping a set of believers and perpetuators. Parsons views these value patterns as not only involved in cultural group actions and attitudes but also as being integrated within personality systems as well.[23] Parsons, however, does warn that these are ideal types which cannot explain marginal cases.[24]

Parsons and White maintain that while the mode of projecting the core values on the part of individuals and groups has changed significantly, there has been little evidence of any great weakening of majority groups or individuals within those majority groups regarding their support of these core values.[25] Thus, since the economic methods of production have changed from that of individualistic, entrepreneurial and self-made man type economies to those of giant corporations and conglomerates, the groups and individuals holding values within the core patterns have shifted in the specific manner in which they project these values. Instead of revealing behavior indicative of Protestant, individualistic, materialistic achievement, emphasis today is placed on achieving success as defined by the corporation owners, the industrial peer group, and managerial college-age groups. Achievement and success as cultural values of the core patterns have simply shifted to a slightly different mode of expression; they have not been eroded to any considerable degree by the variant values of the non-core groupings.[26]

George D. Spindler tends to agree in general with Linton's concept of a solid core of values existing for the other groups.[27] Spindler, however, labels these values as "traditional values" and "emergent values."[28] The traditional values are viewed generally as those expressive of an older American way of life. They emphasize hard work, materialism, high moral standards, etc.; whereas the emergent values as seen by Spindler emphasize togetherness, relativistic morality, sociality, etc.[29] He suggests that much of the hippie or counter-culturalist movement in which individuals or groups tend to espouse group uniformity and group feeling is expressive of the emergent values.[30] It is noteworthy that one witnesses many youngsters today in the junior high and senior high schools acting in such a manner as to indicate their acceptance of emergent-type cultural values.[31] Thus, conflict is inevitable. Younger teachers may, with certain groups of students, hold extremely liberal political ideas and simultaneously proclaim the emergent values as the true ones to be taught and acted upon.[32] Frequently, the methods of teaching are largely indicative of the values being accepted. The "rap session" is usually indicative of emergent values. To the contrary, many older teachers and groups of middle-class students may adhere to the traditional values. While it is merely speculative, it may be suggested that grades received by students and the social status of students within the schools may relate directly to the degree of agreement between the cultural value orientations of students and teachers. Where such orientations are relatively similar, we may expect to find high levels of job satisfaction and student morale, and where great divergence exists between the value orientations we may expect to find low student morale and low teacher job satisfaction. Similarly, the amount of social disorder and chaos existent within the school system, if we are to accept Linton's theory, relates directly to the degree of congruence between the value orientations of educators and students. Thus, in the school system of small towns in relatively isolated areas, we may well find a high level of congruence; likewise, in large urban areas containing a great diversity of cultural groups, we may expect to find low levels of congruence.

Since it is within the nature of cultural groups to feel that their particular set of cultural values and value orientations is the essential and correct one, failure to comply with such cultural value demands will result in some form of punishment from the group. The group also tends to use some form of reward to encourage acceptance of its cultural values. Such rewards or punishments are called sanctions. Negative sanctions are administered for failure to comply with cultural value patterns accepted by the group. Such sanctions, whether negative or positive, may be financial, psychological, physical, etc. Again, educators should be aware of their own tendencies to administer sanctions to students who comply with or rebel against the teacher's value orientation.

In order to obtain a clearer understanding of cultural values and value orientations and thereby be more able to analyze one's own behavior and attitudes as well as those of others involved in the educational processes, let us discuss in some detail the value systems outlined by the Kluckhohns and by Spindler.

The Kluckhohns' Value Orientation Theory

The Kluckhohns' theory or concept of cultural values suggests that certain problems confront every society.[33] There are, according to the theory, a limited number of such problems that each society must solve. The pattern of solutions or cultural values selected are, therefore, also limited in number. The Kluckhohns' cultural value patterns are called value orientations and are of great importance as conceptual tools for educators in dealing with and attaining an understanding of the various majority and minority groups that exist within the school situation. The value orientations held by any particular group such as blacks, Mexican-Americans, immigrants from Appalachia, or proper Bostonians differ significantly and are largely the result of variation in early childhood socialization processes produced within the divergent groups. These value orientations or patterns are behavioral and attitudinal. They compose the total set of rights and wrongs within specific problem dimensions faced by the group. These value orientations or patterns are expressed not only in the home and the church, but also by the children arriving at school who express these attitudes and behaviors in their relationship to the learning situation. The value orientations held by the individual or the group tend to indicate the degree to which social integration into the greater culture has occurred.

According to the Kluckhohns' theoretical concept, all the groups in any social system must decide on the basis of their cultural past and their present life experience how to solve the fundamental problems of dealing with nature, other men, space, time, etc. The Hindu in India may decide on one value orientation in dealing with his relationship to nature, while the industrialized U.S. citizen may decide on quite another solution to his relationship to nature. All societies, however, must, in one manner or another, come to grips with a solution on how they as a group will live and exist alongside nature. The particular set of solutions to the constant problems confronted by all men in all societies is referred to as a value orientation. A knowledge of the particular value orientations likely to be held by large and small groups within the modern community can be of tremendous help to educators who work with children, especially educational administrators who must work in the area of policy formation within the broad general community.

One of the major problems confronted by all men in all societies is that of dealing with and solving the problem of how they work with and associate with other men within the society. This may be translated as the problem of government. According to the Kluckhohns' theoretical framework, there are a limited number of possible ways in which groups and individuals handle or solve this problem. The specific solution they select largely depends upon the cultural heritage that has been passed on to them (early childhood socialization in the home and group) and later life experience. Three possible orientations exist for societies in solving the problem of man's relationship to man, i.e., government. These are (1) linealism; (2) collateralism; and (3) individualism.[34] This area of value orientations tends to raise the question of who shall make the decisions within the group or society. It is possibly the most important of all the values in cultures. Certainly modern man considers it to be very important. The question of which orientation is to be taught is the overriding issue in almost all textbooks and class discussions. The assigned novel in the schoolroom often deals with this subtle question. In short, because value orientations are a part of the cultural learning, the question as to which choice the group or the individual should take is highlighted in many areas of school work. Of course, the child of a particular minority group may be receiving very different answers at home and in his local neighborhood from those being projected by the teacher and texts. In such an instance cultural conflict may be said to exist.

Since three possible choices exist, the educational system, family, and neighborhood groups will tend to emphasize one of the three. On occasion with some groups, the choice will be identical for each of the population units which the student encounters; he, therefore, has no difficulty in absorbing and incorporating that particular idea of man's relationship to man within his personality. To the contrary, since all such population units may not be in agreement, and the student absorbs from the different groups value orientations that are quite different, he may be said to be in culture conflict. Let us examine the three possible choices to which he may orient himself.

Some groups will be lineal in their value judgment. In this, the family, school, or group tends to look toward a specific man or woman as the leader and the one who is expected to make the correct decisions for all members of the group. Lineality is exemplified by the Chinese, who look to Mao Tse-tung as the decision maker. His little red book becomes something of a bible, and his sayings are regarded as completely authoritative. There is little emphasis on the alternate value orientations, such as individualism. In such cultures where the choice has been made in favor of lineality, the cult of the individual is often regarded as completely deviant behavior. Germany in the late 1800s evolved to the degree that lineality became the national solution for problem solving in matters of government. The Kaiser fulfilled this role until he escaped to Holland at the conclusion of World War I. Following that episode, the German peoples apparently still continued to orient themselves toward the choice of lineality as a solution to their problem of government, or man's relationship to man. The Allies attempted to force another orientation on them in the 1920s through forced acceptance of a Western type constitution. Nonetheless, in 1933 the German peoples again selected a value orientation of lineality as a solution to their problem of how to create a better economy and resume world leadership, and the President of the Republic handed the chancellorship to Adolph Hitler. The Germans opted to handle their leadership problem by escaping from the task themselves and permitting father figures to claim that right. In a similar manner, the Roman Catholic church has generally over the centuries tended to emphasize lineality as the best and most correct solution to the problem of "who shall make the decisions." Popes such as John XXIII have served as exemplary leaders in the lineal value orientation. Likewise, the presidency of Franklin D. Roosevelt in the United States presents a picture of the American people who, in the crisis of the economic depression of 1932 to 1936, opted for a somewhat lineal solution to their problems of government. Again, during the World War II period the Congress and the people, in general, tended to regard the President as Commander in Chief; and in doing so, they indicated a preference for a lineal value orientation as a solution to the problem of "who shall make the decisions."

We may occasionally observe that a degree of lineality exists in the families of the upper social classes in the United States in which a grand old patriarch or matriarch in the family really makes all the vital decisions. One has but to read *Eleanor and Franklin*[35] to realize that Mrs. Roosevelt's cultural conflict resulted from her own drive for individualism as opposed to her mother-in-law's insistence on lineality and tradition. Lineality is often expressed in the governmental structure of educational institutions attended by the upper social classes in America. The headmaster or housemaster in the private boarding schools of New England generally tends to hold the position of lineal figure. And in the not too distant past, lineality existed in the collegiate structure, as evidenced by such powerful presidents as Eliot and Lowell, who governed at the Harvard scene. It is possible that much of the conflict that occurred on college and university campuses in the late 1960s and early 1970s, in which students rioted and made demands for reform of the university administrators, was in actuality cultural conflict, inasmuch as colleges and universities tended to act in a lineal manner in their governing policies in contradistinction to the growing numbers of middle-class students whose total environments emphasized the individual cultural value orientation. The two very different value orientations could not exist easily together. It may be that the university structure and system largely imported from Germany tended to bring with it trademarks of the lineality of that culture. Many present-day university administrators are bent on divesting themselves of this father-figure authority and attempting another value orientation for the institutions of higher learning.

Often lineality is preached in the schools founded by minority groups, past and present, who wish to make their voices and demands heard and who feel that such a structure of values tends to best achieve this purpose. Thus, today, a dominant black man or woman may be seen as the real voice and real leader within the black community, and it is he or she who speaks for the black community with respect to its educational needs. The tendency at the same time is for the textbooks and educational materials produced within the schools of such minority groups to reflect lineality as the correct value orientation.

Not only do religious and racial minorities, but frequently geographic regions also, tend to accept lineality as the proper method of government. The southeastern section of the United States is currently the geographic area most apt to place great merit on lineality. It is not a strange sociological phenomenon but one rooted deeply in many levels of the population. Just as many young Southern boys are taught to address their fathers as "sir," so also is the same type of lineality perpetuated and practiced up and down the entire line of group relationships — both in the schools and in the large community. The novels of Tennessee Williams frequently portray the value orientation of lineality in picturing the culture of an almost modern South.

A second value orientation alternative in the man-to-man relationship problem is that of collateralism. In this value orientation of a culture, there is no great white, black, or yellow father figure who is held up to the population as the voice of government, but rather the group is seen as all-important. The soul brothers and sisters, the tribe, the commune, the WASPS, the fraternity, the union brotherhood, etc., are viewed in their total group membership as being the most important and essential entity, with respect to governmental decision making. The big-brother approach to government as well as the chaos of individualism is seen as undesirable. The group is all-important, and the educational materials used by such groups generally stress the worth of the masses, the people, the idea of group belongingness. Collateralism is a value orientation that tends to express high idealism. An early and classic example of this value orientation is that of the North American Indian, who even today retains much collateralism in his society. Schools on Indian reservations frequently are in cultural conflict because the white, middle-class teacher emphasizes individualism to the Indian youngsters, who, conversely, very often come to school already enculturated in collateralism. Behavior and attitudes of a collateral nature may be punished by the insensitive white, middle-class teacher who holds only individualism to be representative of correct actions. In the ancient powwow, Indians made decisions as a group. It was difficult, once a decision was made, to decide who had been the chief decision maker. In such a culture few were permitted to express individuality or lineality.

In an educational structure such as that of the Soviet Union, collateralism is the value orientation venerated and perpetuated. It is the behavioral goal of Soviet education. Textbooks, reading materials, and audiovisuals emphasize it. The story is told of some years ago when an American woman elementary teacher visited the Soviet Union and was permitted to observe an elementary class in which the students were cutting out paper hearts for Friendship Day, a carry-over from St. Valentine's Day of western Europe. One small girl proceeded to cut out a very different type paper heart from that being done by the rest of the students, who were copying a model designed for the whole class. The American teacher observing the individuality rushed over and commented in a very positive and flattering manner. The Soviet teacher, to the contrary, publicly condemned the girl's efforts and commented that she should have done what the rest of the group were doing. This illustrates the nature of collateralism when it is taught in the classroom. The individual is not important, and indeed, is not wanted.

The lower social classes in the United States often place great stress on collateralism in their family groups and neighborhoods. It behooves teachers and school administrators to recognize this fact and to attempt to work with the individuals and groups from this point of view. Many of the store-front schools organized by elements of the black community often reflect curricula and teaching methodology organized in such a manner as to perpetuate the cultural value orientation of collateralism. There is much reading and singing in unison. On a higher level the "rap session" is often used as a method to forward the goal of collateralism where one must communicate, and to a degree identify, with others. Those who espouse collateralism maintain that only through mass participation and sensitizing can the student reach the true educational goals related to collateralism. Within the black militant groups and their families and schools, the organizational structure often stresses collateralism as a desirable goal in student behavior and attitudes. This appears to be especially true of the Black Muslim and such Chicago groups as the Blackstone Rangers. In order to work effectively within such informal and formal educational structures, one must be able to accept to some extent the social and cultural value orientation of collateralism. Perhaps a need exists for more teaching methods in the institutions of higher learning that clearly illustrate and demonstrate this value as a method of working effectively with such groups.

While collateralism may be viewed as a recent or relatively new development, and as reform demanded by only the newly emerging minority groups, it must be remembered that the value orientation has been taught and practiced by the Mennonites, the Dunkards, and the Moravians for well over 200 years in America. They have practiced it in their homes, schools, and communities and continue to do so with no marked degree of unhappiness or disaster for the groups so oriented.

The third and last alternative that a society may select in its cultural choices on government or decision-making problems is that of individuality. It is the one that is selected by most citizens of the United States in solving the problem of man's relationship to man. Individuality is viewed as the traditional value orientation in this problem area. It is seen as part of the core values of the American society. Individualism stresses the rights of the individual to be very different from the group or from even the governmental leaders themselves. The right to argue and to disagree with others is viewed as all-important. The individual may, therefore, belong to any number of groups; however, his actions in any one group may be quite different and at variance with his actions as a member in another group. He is permitted to be an individual whether in the home, in the school, or in the larger community. Often the family itself will indicate the desirability of each of the children's becoming quite different and pursuing very different types of professional or working careers. Such families often even stereotype the children in an unconscious means of securing individuality; one is good at "his books"; another is a socialite; and a third is a good athlete. Thus individuality is encouraged.

In the classrooms of most American schools, especially those dominated by the white middle-class members, this value orientation is very strongly perpetuated. The teacher stresses individual performance, and through the testing and grading systems, individual rewards. The textbook used and problems discussed often have as their central theme the great individual who stands out against the desires of the group or the masses. The myths of an Abe Lincoln, Woodrow Wilson, or Andrew Jackson, as taught in the schools, tend to emphasize the value orientation of individualism. The man or woman who can stand out from the crowd is the one appreciated. This is a core value. Artistic creativity must be highly individualized. Rugged individualism is not just a political slogan for a portion of the middle-class population but a way of life. Individual responsibility is used to perpetuate this value orientation and is stressed considerably within most public schools. Collateralism, seen as "falling among evil companions" is apt to be discouraged. Such collateral terms as clique, secret sorority, and gang indicate the somewhat negative attitude held by school people toward collateralism as a value orientation. The clique or group is often discouraged by the school itself in many informal ways. The secret sorority, or similar collateral organization, in the high school is openly discouraged. In short, in many ways, teachers and school administrators have set the behavioral goal of their schools as that of individualism without having gone through the process of analyzing the alternatives. Much of this has been done in a very unconscious manner and has been accepted as the right goal without questioning the possible results.

Individuality as a cultural value orientation selected or accepted by a society generally appears to result in high degrees of competition. The individual alone is blamed or praised according to the results of such competition. Only on the individual himself may the negative or positive sanctions be placed. One may well recognize that such stress or strain can lead to personal disorder and to many personal social problems. Mental breakdowns, suicides, etc., are undoubtedly related to the degree of individualism stressed within the society. The core cultural values of the society in the United States often place great stress upon success and leave it to the individual to reach that goal. Many cannot do so.

Just as all groups in a society must resolve the problem of government or man-to-man relationships, according to the Kluckhohns' cultural orientation theory, they must also in one manner or another deal with time. They must decide what is the most significant time dimension. This, of course, does not imply that a group within the culture merely sets about in some rational and formal manner deciding on the time dimension which they feel most appropriate. Instead, the cultural value orientation they possess is largely a result of earlier life experience that their cultural ancestors have had and only partially a result of their own actual experiences. Thus, in Pearl Buck's novel *The Good Earth*,[36] the hero, Wang Lung, attempts to preserve the past as much as possible. The older aunts and uncles in the family are supported. He visits the family cemetery. For the hero of the novel, the past is not only a part of his cultural heritage but acts to guide his actions as a young farmer and as an older merchant prince. To the contrary, in the novel *1984*,[37] the past is largely eliminated and rewritten to coincide with the needs of governmental officials. In our own twentieth-century United States the future is everywhere stressed as being the most desirable value orientation. Nothing is worse than to be considered "old-fashioned" or dependent upon the past. The future orientation is stressed in elections. The business world looks forward with anticipation to next quarter's profits or losses. One waits until his ship comes in, in the not-too-distant future. The future is viewed as holy. Movies attempt to portray life as in *2001*, and insurance companies play on the future orientation of millions of Americans in selling policies. The latest and newest automobile is sought by many, and indeed in order to create the impression that the future has arrived, the automobiles manufactured are said to be 1973s, although they are actually manufactured in 1972. Thus, the dominant cultural value in time orientation is expressed by hastening the future as much as possible. Even in child discipline methods, the cultural value orientation expresses itself for many groups in the United States in that the child is told that Christmas is coming and, unless he is self-controlled, he will find little in his stocking at that holiday season.

Three possible alternative value orientations exist according to the Kluckhohns' theory with respect to the time dimension. These are past, present, and future. Societies that are highly industrialized tend to place stress on the future orientation rather than on the present or past. The Soviet Union, like America, tends to emphasize the future dimension. Their challenge to the West is virtually always stated in terms of the future. Marxian doctrine possesses a predictable picture of the future that is emphasized in most educational systems within the Soviet Union. On the other hand, less industrialized nations, peoples, and groups often stress the present or the past dimension in their time orientations. Minority groups similarly often place great stress upon the present or the past.

The lower social classes in the United States are often present-time oriented in their cultural attitudes and behavior. They think primarily of the here and now. As an example, the family grouping may decide to spend Friday's pay check almost immediately. They purchase a guitar and have a wonderful time over the weekend only to discover, to their surprise, that on Monday morning they do not have school lunch money or possibly bus fare. In short, such a variation of cultural value orientation from that held by the major groups in the community may have very direct implications for teachers and educators within the school system. Teachers themselves, usually from the dominant cultural groups, are heavily future oriented and frequently intolerant of any other value orientation displayed. Teachers often insist on the fulfillment of long-range planning or a future-time orientation on the part of students. Such opposite sets of value orientations may well result in what we call culture conflict for many students whose family and neighborhood backgrounds exist within another time dimension. A student coming from a cultural background that emphasizes the present may, upon being questioned by the teacher, indicate his desire to work on some future paper or assignment and might even assure the teacher that he is doing the job. The teacher, however, may often find that at the completion of the time period, no assignment or project has ever been attempted. Educators often find that the child's cultural orientation is such that only immediate assignments and rewards prove effective in encouraging the learning process. The form of motivation most effective for youngsters from the present-time cultural background is short-term and immediate in nature.

A principal in an elementary school in the southwestern section of the United States some time ago noted that her greatest problem was that few of the Mexican-American families in her community were prepared to send their children to school at the appropriate time when it opened in the fall. Upon calling the mother or father she would discover that the family had not planned ahead sufficiently and had not purchased the required materials or clothing and that the family was therefore compelled to wait until the next pay check arrived in order to send the children to school. Such behavior is usually regarded by the dominant population groups as being evidence of shiftlessness and laziness. However, few in the dominant groups tend to realize that they are not so much witnessing inability to cope with a situation as a difference in cultural value orientation.

The dominant value with respect to time in most American families, and certainly the one represented in the public school systems, is the cultural value of future-time orientation. The middle-class family in suburbia or small-town U.S.A. is usually extremely future oriented. The series of religious holidays is often used as a method of perpetuating this value and inculcating it into the child's socialization process. One must wait and be good for 20 or 30 days until Christmas arrives. One must wait until after the afternoon nap to acquire the desired ice cream from the Good Humor man. In countless ways in the informal educational processes conducted by the family, the middle-class child is taught to value the future rather than the present, or certainly the past. Even in later life, the adult with this cultural value orientation, appears not to enjoy the here and now, but tends to plan ahead for progress and abundance or to avoid crisis and disaster.

The school staff is especially apt to reflect in its planning and work a heavy reliance on cultural value orientations expressive of the future. Most teachers come from or convert to middle-class membership and therefore express the dominant value patterns of this group. As a result, children and families representative of minority groups with different time orientations may often be in conflict with school personnel and school policies. Overt conflict frequently breaks out as a result of such cultural diversity. Hostility will often be evidenced when students with present-time orientations feel teachers and counselors do not spend enough time with them listening to their personal and immediate problems. They frequently feel that much of the curricula that is future or past oriented is irrelevant to them. It has nothing to do with the here, the now, and the in-group. Such is doubtlessly true in many instances, for the teachers and counselors often coming from middle-class backgrounds tend to emphasize long-range career plans for students and feel the need for scholastic preparation for the future rather than for immediate job placement. Such educators are merely reflecting their own cultural value orientations. Future planning that reflects no immediate change and preparation for a Regent's examination which will not take place for two years or more may be viewed as intolerable by students whose value orientation is that of present time.

A final alternate value that some groups may select in the time dimension is that of past orientation. This alternate is somewhat less important than the other two simply because fewer groups tend to embrace it. Occasionally, one finds this value present in upper social class American or British schools. It occasionally exists among private and prep type schools that cater to the members of wealthy, old established families. In this value orientation, the headmasters or housemasters may cite past performances on the part of parents or others as standards of performance for the younger generation. The student must major in the same subject area of his father or relatives. He must attend the same Ivy League university, play football at the same school, etc. Hence, much of his life and educational activities is past oriented.

A third cultural problem confronted by all groups and one having importance to educators, according to the Kluckhohns, is that of the relationship of man to nature.[38] While most people may feel that interest in ecology and concern with preservation of the natural environment is a relatively new thing, all groups in one manner or another relate their societies to nature. The American Indian, both in the past and in the present, has demonstrated a variant value from that of the dominant groups in the society by his close, almost personal, relationship to nature. His gods have been nature gods. The names given to his children by the family have frequently been indicative of some aspect of nature. To the contrary, within some societies nature is viewed as overpowering and irresistible. Should the corn crop be washed out in Afghanistan or the rains destroy a dam in India, it may be that the people throw up their hands in frustration and defeat. They view nature as overwhelming. A third example of man's view of nature is that held by many of the peoples of the Soviet Union, northern Europe, and the United States, in which nature is viewed as controllable and used as a source of energy. Thus, air conditioning produces coolness in the summer, and central heating produces summer in the winter. Men study how to control hurricanes and breed their cattle in such a manner as to produce greater amounts of meat and milk. The particular manner in which a group regards nature is a result of cultural heritage and socialization or acculturation methods in the present. The child within the family, no less than the student at school, soon learns and copies the modes of behavior of the adult world in its relationship to nature.

The Kluckhohns picture three alternative choices in man's relationship to nature: (1) nature over man; (2) man with nature; and (3) man over nature.[39] The third alternative, man over nature, is the one generally held to be true by the American middle class and thus the one most espoused by the teachers and school administrators. Much of the literature taught in the schools emphasizes this orientation. One is repeatedly told in school that he or she has the ability to do the work. All that is required is determination, i.e., man over nature. High achievement is a standard of performance within almost all educational levels. The four-minute mile can be run; indeed, it has been. The student who has overcome some natural handicap is the one who is cited and lauded by teachers and school administrators. The notion that, irrespective of

I.Q. or inherited ability, one can be made educable is deeply embedded in the school's philosophy.

To the contrary, especially among some minorities and lower social class groups, there has existed the value orientation of nature over man. In this view, the individual or group is subject to nature. He can do little to overcome the problem. He must submit: "What will be will be." If, indeed, a window is broken in the tenement house, it is likely to remain so. There exists for those who are oriented toward nature over man a feeling of hopelessness and helplessness in overcoming the obstacles placed before them in society. The crippled child is probably allowed to remain crippled within this cultural orientation. The child "who cannot learn" is accepted as such by the parents within this orientation. To the contrary, this particular orientation, when expressed by an individual to the teacher, is frequently met with extreme indignity. The person possessing this value is considered a defeatist and often rejected by most major groups holding other value orientations.

A third alternative, and one increasingly voiced as the correct orientation by the hippie or counter-culturalist groups as well as by many scientists, is that of man with nature. Here the group views man as cooperating with nature. They appear as a team. Man does not destroy nature and then attempt to recreate it, as expressed in the orientations of those believing in man over nature, but holds nature to be his equal. Perhaps it is easiest to exemplify this value orientation in a foreign culture such as that of old Japan, in which the architecture blended into the natural surroundings in such a manner as to enhance both. *Tea House of the August Moon* reveals this value orientation in the Japanese characters portrayed in the movie. Here the Japanese characters express an intense desire to build a tea house to which they can come in the evening and watch the sun set over the Sea of Japan and enjoy the sunlight and shadows as they flicker through the pine trees. This is man with nature. In the American culture this orientation is relatively new. Attempts to fight pollution and save the redwood forests of California are expressive of this value orientation.

Teachers and school administrators are often products of the middle social class business-oriented communities and may have difficulty tolerating any but their own view, i.e., that of man over nature. However, there appears to be great pressure from those outside the core values to realign the culture toward a more man-with-nature orientation. And it must be remembered that possibly the greatest architect of our time, Frank Lloyd Wright, obviously advocated a man-with-nature approach in his building style. The "waterfall house" and others reflect this orientation.

The fourth area in which common human problems exist and for which all peoples at all times must find some solution is that of work and productivity.[40] In some respects the question raised is that of the distribution of divisions of labor. Within most modern revolutions there has been the implicit and explicit command that all shall work. One has but to view the movie *Doctor Zhivago*[41] to sense the different value orientation being imposed upon the people of the Soviet Union after the revolution. Doing something of value and worth in the world of work became a very definite virtue in the eyes of the revolutionary leaders. Within our own American culture, doing something in the area of work has long been highly valued. The Abe Lincolns boasted of their prowess in logging. The folk heroes such as Paul Bunyon and his Blue Ox emphasize to every schoolchild the desirability of work and high achievement. On the other hand, this is not the particular value orientation of certain cultures. In an older India, it appears that an orientation toward simply being, existing, was generally held by much of the population. One may recall the slogan used by the Indians: "Only Englishmen and mad dogs go out in the noonday sun." One suspects that ambassadors from the United States, oriented toward doing something in the area of work and productivity, frequently become disgusted and despair of the future when they view a foreign people who are not so work oriented and who appear to care little for Alliances for Progress or proposed Five-Year Plans, all of which are based on the premise that the culture is doing-oriented. Often it is not.

The Kluckhohns suggest three possible alternative choices a group may make in the area of work activity. The three alternative choices are (1) doing; (2) being; and (3) being-and-becoming.[42] The dominant groups in the United States are oriented toward the doing value. They place great emphasis on the necessity of a man or group's doing something. He must certainly work at something. The child within the family structure is often given tasks and chores to emphasize the importance of work. The family may purposefully purchase a pet for the child in order that he learn "to take care of the animal." Likewise, in the typical school setting, the teacher places great emphasis on the doing orientation. The teacher often feels that idle hands create discipline problems, and consequently assigns much "busy work" that may later be tossed into the waste basket. The entire world of school sports is oriented around the doing value. The slogan often used by the small town high school senior class reflects this emphasis, with such sayings as "Give Us the Tools to Do the Deed," etc. In fact, the community tends to regulate one's social class membership on the basis of what one's father does as an occupation. The child in the average middle-class family early evidences that the doing orientation has become part of his culture by demanding of his often busy and distraught mother, "What can I do now?" He feels from his acculturation process that he must definitely find something to do. Such a particular value orientation appears to provide the family, school, and community with tremendous motivation and achievement drive. This value orientation usually suggests a very dynamic type society.

To the contrary, some groups in a given society may, through historical accident or present economic position, develop another value orientation in the area of work relations. One such possible alternative is that of a being cultural orientation. The lower social class members in the community often reflect this value in their family-rearing processes and in their behavior within the schools and classrooms. The being orientation is expressed in the thought of "letting things alone." No attempt is made to do much about anything. The being orientation is epitomized by the group or family's sitting on the front porch and enjoying life. To a doing-oriented group or individual this activity is viewed as laziness. However, it must be suggested that the high degree of doing orientation expressed by so many groups in the United States doubtlessly contributes in part to the high degree of mental fatigue, mental problems, etc., existent within the society as a whole. Vacation schedules and intended periods of relaxation are probably mandatory in a culture that places so much stress on doing something and achieving greatness. The hippie groups most clearly today represent an alternative choice in this area of values, since they are often being oriented in their behavior.

A third alternative appears to exist in the area of work values, and this is being-and-becoming.[43] This is viewed as a transitional stage between the doing and being orientations.

The fifth societal problem which all peoples must solve, according to the Kluckhohns' theory, concerns the possessions of the culture. Two alternatives exist in this instance on something of a continuum. The solutions are (1) materialism and (2) spiritualism.[44] It is obvious that most western Europeans, Russians, and Americans have opted for the materialistic solution concerning what it is desirable to possess. Within the Soviet philosophy there is the concept of dialectical materialism or the premise that methods of productivity of materialistic goods are the key determinant in shaping history. Likewise, the speech made by the President of the United States in his State of the Union Message usually delivered before Congress in January is apt to be labeled by the press as "Guns or Butter." Little in either national culture directs itself toward spiritualism. On the other hand, the cultures of the Middle East and Far East are often thought of as extremely spiritualistic in their general philosophies and ways of life. India, with its multitudes of religious sects, is an especially interesting example of a culture that has chosen spiritualism as its most highly prized possession.

Within the United States, it is the middle-class social groups that tend to place the greatest emphasis on materialism. The child is taught in an informal manner in the home to save his pennies, to "take good care" of his articles of clothing and to hang them up, since they have been purchased at high cost, to preserve the furniture and not climb over it, and later to take good care of the car, since it cost a great deal of money. Often the adolescent's good behavior is purchased by means of the allowance. As an adult, he will find that when he gives to the church he can profitably do this because it is discounted on his income taxes.

Since most teachers and school administrators have been reared in, and are members of, the American middle class, they also tend to stress materialism even within their professional behavior in the schools. The student is taught not to write needlessly in his books, not to destroy school property, not to carve on the desks, not to damage books by leaving them in the rain or snow, etc. Frequently, one reads in a magazine or a newspaper advertisement that the advantage of a college education is that the graduate will make $150,000 more in his lifetime than if he does not possess the sheepskin. In short, educational achievement is measured in terms of materialism in many homes. It is not exceptional to witness money being given to the senior upon graduation by his family.

The typical curricula offered in high schools indicate also a concern with materialism. Business-type education courses are offered on how to invest money, how to account for money spent or saved, how to sell materialistic products, etc. Banking and finance are often offered, along with business law. The school frequently serves the interests of the business community to a very great extent.

The social status of particular students within the schools often relates directly to the amount of materialism that can be displayed by them or their parents. The "show and tell" exercises usually held in the elementary grades are examples of the permeation of materialistic culture orientation within the school systems.

While the lower social classes do not differ significantly from the middle classes in their value placed on materialism, they certainly possess less of it. However, it is the hippie or counter-cultural group and their value orientations that display a variation on the cultural choice; and in general they have chosen spiritualism over materialism. Indeed, one may witness, on occasion, this same choice by many youngsters of the modern generation. Occasionally, such variation of choices within the same family lends itself to a generation gap with respect to values, behaviors, and attitudes. This opposite choice, or spiritualism, is indicated by a concern with brotherhood, sharing of wealth, concern with the occult, anti-war demonstrations, etc.

It is perhaps wise to note that spiritualism does not indicate a great concern with formalized religion but may consist simply of a non-materialistic type philosophy. Thus, art appreciation or music appreciation may well be defined as spiritualistic in nature. Doubtlessly, it is wise for teachers and school administrators to examine and reexamine the curricula and the school rules to determine the proper amount of materialism and spiritualism that should be introduced. Should they prefer something more of a balance than is currently exhibited, they should move to make the needed changes. Again, the choices that the school personnel make do, in the long run, affect the entire community and national culture.

The final value orientation theorized by the Kluckhohns is that of determining the nature of and evaluating the innate capacities of man.[45] In short, this orientation asks the question of what is the basic nature of man. Some societies suggest in their cultural interpretations that man is born evil.[46] This is indicated by early Puritan groups who believed in severe discipline in the home, church, and school. Frequently, students were hanged by their thumbs for misbehavior. The dunce's cap and dullard's stool were invented by this type of cultural group. On the other hand, some societies culturally define the child as being born basically good.[47] The oriental cultures tend to hold this to be true and educate their children accordingly. The French philosopher Jean-Jacques Rousseau obviously held this to be the case and wrote his *Emile*[48] with this concept in mind. Finally, the American culture, along with many northern European cultures, has evolved from a philosophy which purports that the child is born evil (as maintained by the Puritans) but is nevertheless perfectible.[49] Thus, in the home and school the adults are usually rather severe in discipline, but do acknowledge that the child is capable of improvement. Many of the school laws on corporal punishment and discipline relate directly to this cultural concept.

The value orientation in the area of how man is born is currently shifting rapidly. Some national figures call for a return to earlier concepts, while others merely request that the currently held evil-but-perfectible idea be implemented. Nonetheless, it may well be suspected that the value orientation of the child's being born good and therefore not especially subject to any, and certainly not harsh, discipline is coming to prevail. One again views some semblance of a generation gap in this matter, with the fifty-years-and-older group wanting more severe discipline, whereas younger groups may view this as medieval behavior.

The Spindler Value Structure

Having expounded at some length on the value orientations designated by the Kluckhohns, let us turn to the system of values suggested by George D. Spindler.[50] An examination of this second system may provide the educator with additional insight into the concept of culture and its relationship to educational structure and function. Spindler theorizes that many of the difficulties presently experienced in today's world can best be explained as a result of transformation of the core values within the general American culture.[51] He suggests that we are presently observing a radical shift in the core values held by the citizens, and this shift is especially evident among young adults.[52]

Spindler pictures the society as sharply split between those individuals and groups who hold the older or more traditionalist type values and those who, often young, espouse a newer set of values which he labels as emergent values.[53] The educator is, according to this theory, especially subject to problems evolving out of this shift of core values.[54] This transformation and consequent split in core values is frequently evidenced by the difficulty experienced in obtaining even the slightest degree of consensus on solutions to major issues. Thus, a large-city superintendent of schools such as that in Philadelphia or any other major city attempts to work with one group, only to discover that he has alienated another equally important group. His being fired often follows close upon the heels of his being hired. Members of minority groups may make certain demands upon him, whereas members of the majority groups become alienated if he gives in on the minority demands. To be a successful superintendent he must secure the support and agreement of both elements, and they are absolutely divided on the basic cultural core values.

Spindler suggests that the shift in core values is most clearly evidenced by the selection of types of personality thought to be desirable by those individuals and groups whom he has studied over the past several years.[55] Among those espousing the older or more traditionalist values, the personality characteristics cited as being most desirable are individuality, originality, creativity, achievement, and success.[56] Among those individuals and groups who have shifted in their core values, Spindler has found that the desired personality orientations are toward sociability, extroversion, concern for others, conformity to the group, and hedonism.[57] While there appear to be no absolute lines concerning the types of groups or individuals who hold the emergent or traditional type values, it may be said in general that the younger generation has tended to espouse the emergent values to a greater extent than the older generation. This, in part, may account for much of the generation gap so clearly evidenced in today's society. Faculties and other groups of educational personnel, so it is suggested by Spindler, may also be divided along this sociological continuum, with certain groups, such as school boards, school administrators, and older teachers, tending to hold the more traditionalist values, whereas younger teachers, some groups of students, and some parents may hold emergent values.[58] The traditionalists may view their colleagues and other educators who hold the emergent type values as being "pink," slightly Communistic, way-out, hippies, etc.[59] To the contrary, the teachers and others holding the emergent type value may regard their colleagues with traditionalist type values as "old-fashioned," squares, and possibly even Fascists.[60]

Spindler labels the important traditional values as (1) Puritan morality, (2) work-success ethic, (3) individualism, (4) achievement orientation, and (5) future time orientation. He suggests the emergent values to be (1) sociability, (2) relativistic morality, (3) consideration for others, (4) hedonistic, present-time orientation, and (5) conformity to the group.[61] Many of these values closely resemble those spelled out by the Kluckhohns and need little further explanation; however, a few values representative of the traditional and emergent orientations and not previously dealt with will be outlined in a brief manner in order to give the reader a more thorough understanding of the relationship of culture to educational structure and process.

The work-success ethic as proposed by Spindler represents the belief and attitude that one can get ahead in this world, if he really tries, that there is a good job for every good man, that one must "get up off his rear and get moving," and that to fail is really just an indication of laziness and shiftlessness on the part of the individual or group.[62] Welfare programs are seen as giveaways. This particular value, held by the traditionalists, emphasizes much of the older Puritan-Protestant ethic originally formulated by Max Weber.[63] Emphasis is placed upon work as being almost holy. Indeed, one can, according to certain Protestant doctrine, virtually secure admission into heaven through good deeds or by doing a great amount of the right type work. Work is viewed as pleasurable. Doubtlessly, those educators who hold this value to a high degree will espouse in their educational programs the necessity of the children's earning their grades and privileges. It can be hypothesized that teachers who hold the traditional values to a high degree will emphasize stern discipline and will act as taskmasters. They will most likely indicate the "life ain't no crystal stairs" theme in their approach to teaching. Homework, and a great deal of it, will be stressed in the traditionalist's classroom teaching and administrative capacity. One suspects that he is listening to a traditionalist when he hears a former student comment that the best teachers in the high school were those who made him work the hardest—that old Miss Battle-Ax was his best teacher.

A second value held by the traditionalist is that of Puritan morality.[64] Abstention, respectability, reputation, duty, delayed gratification, and sexual restraint are seen by Spindler as core values of the traditionalists.[65] Educators who hold traditionalist values will be seen as absolutely opposed to the introduction of sex classes into the school system's curricula. They view the introduction of such classes as simply "putting ideas" into the heads of students. School laws and regulations devised by the traditionalists frequently emphasize that "the good school citizen" does not display affection in public. In short, no hand-holding, no kissing, or worse is permitted. Traditionalists have frequently written the rules prohibiting attendance at school by pregnant students. Under such traditionalist rules, married students are not permitted to participate in varsity school athletics. They view these behaviors or conditions as signs of degeneracy in the school population. Not infrequently, awards presented at an honors convocation display traditionalist oriented values. Those students named or elected best school citizen or honored for school leadership tend to be those individuals who most closely identify with the older, more traditionalist, type values. James Coleman has discovered that many factors considered by the teachers holding traditionalist type values to be important are not similarly regarded as particularly important by the student themselves.[66]

The third value especially emphasized by the traditionalists is that of achievement orientation.[67] The educators who hold this value as part of their cultural orientation do not usually permit their students to "rest upon their laurels." Students are frequently urged to their utmost limits. Often included in the regularly assigned examinations are questions of such difficulty that no student in the class is likely to be able to answer them. The teacher of traditionalist values is, therefore, satisfied that she has truly measured the academic limits of her students. Athletes are urged by the traditionalists to go all-out. The school personnel, guided by traditionalists, expect to go all-out to win the game on Saturday. Pep rallies will be held. Indeed, a prayer to God, if it is deemed helpful, will be offered up prior to the team's going on the court or field. No possible source of help is to be rejected. Many teachers regard high professional achievement on the part of their students in later life as the supreme accomplishment of their own teaching career.

To the contrary, Spindler suggests that emergent values are espoused frequently by large portions of the student body and by many of the younger teachers.[68] Thus, the school population is frequently split on value orientations and, therefore, divided on just about everything else. One of the characteristic qualities of those holding emergent values is that of the hedonistic, present-time orientation.[69] This value expresses itself in an attitude of eat, drink, and be merry, for who can foretell the future, and besides who is very concerned about it with the way things are today? I might to to war and be killed; so, therefore, I need not study tonight. The carefree attitude is the best one. The "here," "the now," the "Pepsi generation," and the happy-go-lucky attitude is the important thing.

Another value emphasized by the emergent group is that of conformity to the group.[70] Responses indicative of this value are that it is better to be popular than to be a class brain, it is nice to be smart but it is smarter to be nice, to be outstanding is to be considered an "apple polisher" by the group, and the "in group" is the really status thing to belong to in the school. Conformity to the group produces stress on adhering to the dress code of the "in group," not necessarily that of the establishment as set up by teachers and school administrators.

Spindler suggests that it is quite probable that the present teaching population has been reared and socialized within traditionalist type homes.[71] They may, therefore, tend to be heavily influenced by traditionalist values and therefore emphasize them in their roles as teachers. It appears that culture conflict may be created when and if student teachers, possibly possessing emergent type value orientations, should be assigned to traditionalist type cooperating teachers. Should the student teacher under such circumstances express his values in the teaching situation, difficulties may predictably arise. On the other hand, where value orientations of student teachers and cooperating teachers are quite similar, we will find excellent cooperation and high mutual praise.

One observes today the situation in which student bodies on many university and college campuses are sharply split with respect to value orientations. While there appears to be a transformation of the core values held by the students in favor of the emergent patterns, it is not unusual to find in certain geographic areas that, while the student government officers and newspaper editors hold emergent values, the majority of the student body still continues to hold traditionalist values. The latter often and publicly proclaim that the student government and newspaper do not represent them; and in truth, in some instances, they do not. Another case demonstrating a conflict of values is that presently existent on a small black university campus in the state of Louisiana in which a black traditionalist president is being bitterly opposed by a black student body with emergent values.

The Concept of Cultural Lag

A concept of use to sociologists of education and educators alike is that of cultural lag. William F. Ogburn has been especially productive in his work with this sociological concept.[72] Basic to the concept of cultural lag is the idea that the various elements of a society's culture do not evolve or change at the same rate of speed. Thus, many of the mechanical innovations of present-day America change and are modified relatively easily and quickly. The TV set is outmoded in a very brief period of time, as is the family automobile. To the contrary, habits and attitudes on the part of the population often change slowly. The prison system dates back to the fifteenth and sixteenth centuries, and the specifics of prison life have changed but little since then. However, we have landed on the moon by inventing and improving upon a set of highly complex mechanical devices. In order to achieve this latter goal, the culture has allocated great amounts of the national resources. The urge to catch up with the Soviet Sputnik project produced rapid and enormous change within the scientific areas of the culture; however, the population has permitted an electoral system for selecting the President to persist despite the fact that it is outmoded and may create enormous problems in the future. In short, elements of the culture have not proceeded to change at the same rate of speed.[73] Knowledge of man's social behavior, information on ecological controls, and human productivity are little advanced as compared with many other areas of human endeavor.

Within the world of education, cultural lag creates many problems. Just at a time when many minority groups seek entry of their members into the professions, many of the majority groups already within the professions are attempting to raise the certification requirements for entry. Thus, just as many blacks and other minority groups have become conscious of their need for entering the mainstream of American life, such professions as that of nursing are pressing hard to raise the requirements for admission. The nursing profession appears desirous of abolishing the older two- and three-year diploma programs and establishing in their place the four-year college degree program. This is evidence of cultural lag within education. The two elements within the society appear to be in different time zones. There is apparently little communication between them. Results of this nature create many social problems and produce a lack of cohesiveness within the general culture.

Another example of cultural lag in the educational situation is that in which parents and community citizens often refuse to acknowledge the need for sex education within the school curricula. It is undoubtedly true that in an earlier agrarian period little such formal education was needed. The child was very aware of life, procreation, and death through his personal and direct experience in working with the livestock on the farm. Today, many parents still view this as the natural and logical method of teaching sex education, i.e., the family takes the responsibility for the sex education. However, today the farm family has largely disappeared. It has been replaced by a highly industrialized urban type family environment, and the child is almost never able to gain the experience and knowledge earlier obtained by the farm boy or girl. Yet, the parents hold attitudes formulated in an earlier period that are no longer appropriate to the situation.

Cultural lag is further evidenced in the schools by the fact that in many schools married students are restricted in the amount of freedom they are permitted with respect to academic and athletic participation. In many areas, pregnant girls are not permitted to attend school, and married students may not participate in varsity athletic competition. Such policies are based on earlier Puritan philosophies that are no longer accepted by the general public or supported by medical fact. Sociologists of education label policies of this nature as cultural atavism.

Another more common example of cultural lag is that involving the organization of the school calendar. The usual school calendar reflects an economic situation that no longer exists and has not existed for almost 50 years. Summer vacations were originally designed so that children might aid their parents in the farm work of planting and harvesting. Such child labor was absolutely essential to maintain the economic welfare of the family. Today, a very small percentage of students need provide such labor. The population is largely urban and even on the farm the process of mechanization has largely eliminated the need for unskilled child labor. Yet, the school schedules have usually not been brought up to date. Few school administrators or school boards have even attempted to experiment with the calendar as a method for producing greater learning among the students.

Negative and Positive Sanctions in Education

Another concept within the framework of cultural theory of use to educators is that of sanctions. Sanctions are the rewards or punishments that help to establish social control within the culture. A culture establishes certain norms as the correct types of attitudes and behaviors within the society. Sanctions are used to persuade members of the group to conform to the norms established within the culture. Failure to comply with norms often leads to some form of psychological or physiological punishment. To the contrary, the group frequently uses some form of positive sanctions such as rewards to encourage the acceptance of the norms established within the culture. It is interesting to note that among families and neighborhoods, known as primary groups, the sanctions may be highly informal, i.e., spankings, restrictions on freedom to do something or purchase something on the part of the child, a "talking to," teasing, or being told that one is not likely to go to heaven for his misdemeanors. In the larger societies particular agencies known as secondary groups, schools, churches, government bureaus, etc., often administer negative or positive sanctions that are highly formal in nature. Thus, within the educational system, a secondary group, the positive sanctions may be represented by such rewards as scholarships to colleges and universities, a DAR Nursing scholarship, a letter of a complimentary nature being sent by the principal to the student's parents, by the listing of names on the honor role, by election to National Honor Society, etc. On the other hand, in the school system negative sanctions are frequently represented by the processes of probation, expulsion, physical discipline, exclusion, and isolation.

The primary aim of sanctions is to produce conformity, solidarity, and continuity within the cultural grouping. It is one of the most basic methods of social control possessed by educators. Negative sanctions are generally used to prevent individuals from disturbing the classroom or school activities. Usually, the negative and positive sanctions that are likely to be administered for particular forms of deviant behavior are well known by the school's population. This knowledge, if formalized, is usually called a code. Each academic generation has its own code and enforces it; thus, social control is maintained and cultural continuity is preserved. However, in the rapidly changing and often chaotic society in which we live, the code held as official by a school's population may come into conflict with the informal codes held by students who may be suddenly bussed in from other cultural areas. Consequently, it becomes difficult for students, teachers, and school administrators to formulate rules and regulations acceptable to a substantial majority of the student population. Officials in a rapidly changing neighborhood school may find great difficulty in devising a set of negative and positive sanctions acceptable for any length of time. The cultural groups composing the school population may be changing at such a rate of speed as to produce the previously cited condition of cultural lag. Old sanctions become inappropriate for the new groups, and as a result, the social controls within the school tend to deteriorate.

Mores and Education

Another concept of use to the sociologists of education and educators is that of mores. Mores are often confused with morals; while in some instances they may be quite similar, they are not always identical. Mores are identified with the untouchables of the culture. One almost never thinks of violating the mores of the society. They are ingrained in our individual personalities. The teacher may become irritated with the lack of air conditioning in her classroom. She might toy with the thought of wearing short-shorts; however, she would never think of going nude to school as a solution to the heat problem. Dating one's own students is generally forbidden, and so strongly is it instilled in the system that it need not be written down or codified in any manner. It is a part of the mores of the academic community and needs no codification. Another violation of the mores of a community was illustrated some time ago on an evening news program. An elementary male school principal, a respected and married member of the community, had undergone surgery to produce a sex change. He had become an anatomical female. He dressed as a female. He and his wife maintained that this was his personal privilege and had nothing to do with his professional behavior as an elementary principal. The community appeared to think otherwise.

The educator must be especially aware of the mores of the general community in which he holds office. The mores set the outer limits for his attitudes and behaviors. To violate the mores of the community is to breach the most internalized set of values of the culture. Such violation is almost surely to cost the educator his position in the school system.

Folkways and Education

The final concept of special relevance for educators discussed in the present chapter is that of folkways. Folkways and mores are both sets of social norms or forms of social control. Folkways, however, do not carry the extreme severity of meaning that is characteristic of mores. Violation of folkways may be condemned, but will not often result in severe punishment. The principal should wear a tie and jacket to school according to the folkways of many communities. Failure to do so may be considered improper, but not evil, behavior. Such behavior may result in his being informally told what is expected by his subordinates, teachers and students, or by his superordinates, associate superintendents or the superintendent. The students should not address the teacher by his or her first name in a formal classroom setting; however, a tendency on the part of the students to do so usually results in only minor negative sanctions being applied.

The educator is freer to challenge the folkways of the community than its mores. He may suggest that it would not really hurt to alter the folkway behavior in question. Folkways generally tend to simply represent the most diplomatic or acceptable way of dealing with a particular situation within a specific community. Violators of folkways are considered thoughtless, impolite, or brash, but not criminal. Educators must be able to clearly distinguish between the community's folkways and mores.

CHAPTER 3

Concepts of Social Stratification and Their Relevance for Education

Defining Social Class

Sociology of education has from its inception placed very great emphasis upon the concept of social stratification. More work has been done in analyzing the relationship between education and systems of social stratification than in almost all other areas of sociology of education combined. A review of textbook materials reveals that almost one-third of the space used in exploring and explaining sociology of education is devoted to concepts involving social stratification. One enterprising author undertook to analyze the types of research done in the general area and discovered that 333 studies had been on social stratification in one eight-year period alone.[1] Lloyd Warner, Allison Davis, Robert Havighurst, and August Hollingshead early evidenced an interest in social stratification.[2] Such individuals as Bernard Barber, R. Bendix and S. Lipset, Gerhard E. Lenski, Harold Pfautz, D. C. MacRae, C. W. Mills, P. Hatt, Joseph S. Roucek, and N. Rogoff have made significant contributions to the theory of social stratification in the post-World War II period.[3] While many present-day sociologists of education tend to rely heavily upon concepts of social stratification as a major part of their lecture and discussion materials, earlier men and women in the teaching field tended to emphasize it to an even greater degree. It often serves as the "meat and potatoes" of any course in sociology of education.[4]

Social stratification as a concept may refer to almost any size population unit, ranging from small groups to the general society. However, in any system of social stratification, individuals and groups are ranked in such a manner as to create inequality with respect to privileges, power, and prestige.[5] Members of the group or society are arranged in relatively permanent ranks with respect to their statuses (jobs, political positions, talents and skills, family ancestry, racial and ethnic origins, or other factors) within a system.[6] There are several types of social stratification. Among these are social classes, castes, church hierarchies, racial groupings, governmental positions in civil service systems, etc.; however, practically always sociologists of education, in referring to the concept, tend to mean social classes. Social class structure, as has been noted, is only one form of social stratification, but it is the most important one and the most frequently studied.

Briefly, a social class is a division of people in society who have relatively similar backgrounds with respect to wealth, education, and occupational status. Persons and groups composing a particular social class have many things in common with regard to shared values, attitudes, behaviors, and dispositions. They tend to form a predictable pattern in their life-style, which distinguishes them from members of other social classes. Increasingly, they tend to share the same life space with others of the same social class. They are linked together not only in behavior and attitudes, but also in shared geographic areas. Thus, suburbia increasingly tends to reflect the life-style of only one or two social classes. Likewise, the inner city may be the abode of one or two social classes. Particular social classes may be more oriented toward certain political parties than to others and tend to vote on a social class membership basis. Politicians frequently refer to such a phenomenon as "block voting." Particularly in the Protestant world, a specific religious denomination may have greater appeal for members of one social class than for members of another. Thus, a particular branch of the Protestant church may reflect the values and attitudes of the social class which supports it and constitutes a majority of its membership. It is basically this sense of sameness and belongingness that is the underlying ingredient of social class membership.

Those behavioral scientists who are followers of Karl Marx's theories regard social class structures as being primarily based on economic factors. They hold that the divisions of social class structures are related to and determined by the economic means of production and distribution within the society. According to this view, citizens within an industrial type economy do not place equal value on all occupational positions. The positions are arranged in the manner of a pyramid, with those occupations central to the running and control of industrial production (owners and managerial staffs) located at the very top or apex of the pyramid. These positions are held by a relatively few people in the society, and their occupants receive great wealth, power, and prestige. Those people who occupy a position near the base of the industrial pyramid, while working long and hard hours, perform tasks not considered to be especially valuable to the general society and thus reap little material wealth and have negligible power within the total society. The Marxists suggest that conflict between the people on the base, the proletariat, and the people in the middle and top, the bourgeoisie, is inevitable, and proclaim the rights of those at the base to have greater economic rewards and voice in policy formation.[7] Basically, the Marxists view social class membership as economic and usually discuss it in only economic terms.

Other sociologists and sociologists of education have suggested that social class membership cannot be attributed to one single factor, but rather indicate that it is based on a composite of factors such as family environment, wealth, cultural ancestry, occupational status (type of job held in society), racial identity, etc.[8] This latter group usually refers to these composite factors under the wholesale terms of life-styles and life-chances. Thus, individuals or groups in the community with similar life-styles belong to the same social class. The divisions that separate the different social classes in any society are at best difficult to determine. Some sociologists and sociologists of education tend to measure social class membership from a subjective point of view. The individual is presented with descriptions of several social classes within his community. He is asked to identify which he most closely resembles with respect to life-style. Other behavioral scientists measure social class membership from a more objective point of view. They establish certain patterns of characteristics for each social class division, and after using interviews, questionnaires, or observation methods, fit the individuals or groups into specific divisions within the community.[9]

Again, there is much difficulty presented in attempting to delineate social classes within any specific community. The critics of most theories of social class patterns have been quick to point out that many communities do not have the same social classes present in each of them. There appear to be some differences in social class divisions and size of social classes, depending upon the region of the country being examined and upon the size of the urban area studied. Small towns and villages may have only four or five social classes, whereas large urban areas may have six. Geographically, it is suggested that the northern region of the United States tends to contain more upper social class members than the Midwest. The tremendous amount of geographic mobility evidenced in large portions of the population also renders difficult the study of social class structure. It is relatively easy to analyze social class divisions in stable or primitive societies; however, American society is neither.

In an earlier period of American history, most citizens refused to accept the concept of social class divisions. Many felt that in a frontier society, all were potentially equal, inasmuch as each possessed the same life-chances. There was an abundance of life space. Since the economic depression of 1929-39 most Americans have become increasingly aware of social class divisions and the fact that all do not have equal life-chances, despite Constitutional guarantees that suggest they do. Many have become aware that accident of birth does affect one's opportunities. The wealth, power, and prestige of being born a Kennedy, a Rockefeller, a Stevenson, a Roosevelt, a Taft, or a Byrd have not gone unnoticed by the general public. The work of such men as Vance Packard in his *The Status Seekers* has made many conscious of differences in social class attitudes and behaviors;[10] however, there still exists much folklore of the Horatio Alger type that attempts to deny the existence and importance of social class membership.

While most Americans have come to accept the concept of social class divisions, they hold certain principles as necessary in the functioning of the system. The first principle is that the social class system must be open rather than closed.[11] Individuals and groups must have the right to change their positions to the degree that their talents and abilities permit. This is basically written into all government documents and accepted within all popular political philosophies. The structure must be viable. Most people in the country have insisted that this is one of the primary tasks of the schools. It appears that they believe, wisely or unwisely, that chief responsibility for maintaining an open class society should be in the hands of educators. Thus, according to much popular opinion, the educators should manage their school programs in such a manner as to not only permit but also to aid students in developing talents sufficient to permit their rising in the social class system. The educators are expected to provide the students capable of upward mobility not only with the technical skills and knowledge but also with manners, behaviors, attitudes, and general life-styles which are needed for upward social mobility.

There are varying degrees to which social class systems are open or closed. Traditionally, such systems have been more nearly closed in European societies than has been true generally for the American scene. India manifests a still more closed social class structure which is referred to as a caste system. In short, the closed system or caste system does not permit social mobility for individuals or groups. If one is born into the caste of the Brahmans, Kshatriyas, Vaisyas, Sudra, etc., he will receive an education appropriate to the occupational tasks for which members of the caste are responsible. The individual will marry a wife who is also a member of his caste, and his life will be lived out in the life-style of all members of his caste. On the other hand, Americans have ideologically opted for an open system wherein all may attempt to achieve as high a position in the social stratification system as possible. Teachers, professors, counselors, and school administrators have usually accepted this concept of upward social mobility as basic to the code of teacher training and teaching ethics. The public has generally expected them to implement it.

A second principle held by most Americans is that rewards for those at the top of the social class scale may be much greater than for those at the bottom.[12] This, of course, is basic to a capitalistic system. The public has generally placed differential values upon the work tasks in the society, and those of greatest expertise, the top-level business and professional positions, are regarded as the most valuable and, therefore, deserving of the greatest rewards. These positions require special knowledge and long periods of training that can only be provided within formal educational structures. Thus, increasingly as Warner and others noted, the educational institutions are one of the few means of social mobility for many individuals and groups in the society.[13] Such institutions alone have the equipment and know-how to provide many with the knowledge and skills essential for occupying the top-of-the-ladder positions. The actual shape or structure of the social class system wherein there may be many on the bottom and few at the top has been of no great concern to Americans as long as they believe that the system is an open one permitting any to rise in it.[14] Textbooks used in most educational institutions in the United States have for the past 100 years tended to stress the theme of the poor boy rising to the top. The story of men rising from the log cabin to the White House is a common theme in most U.S. history books.

A third principle accepted by most Americans is that, within the system of social stratification, those on the lower levels of the system will accept the legitimacy of the system.[15] They are expected to accept the status quo and not attempt to change to any appreciable degree the establishment or system that provides for the inequality of rewards. No open rebellion must take place. Perrucci has suggested that, where the individuals or groups on the lower levels do not accept these conditions or deny the legitimacy of the system, social problems will be evident.[16] Almost all textbooks used in teaching in the schools of the United States appear to attempt to legitimize the system. Hence, this may be one of the reasons for so much criticism by minority groups of the functions of the public schools. They view the schools as being married to and supportive of the social class system.[17] One suspects that the militant blacks tend to hold the schools responsible for supporting a system which they sometimes find oppressive and one in which they are almost always located on the bottom. One frequently hears such complaints in the phrase that "the system is bad." Those who support the social stratification system and its differential system of rewards usually do so by referring to things such as "the American way of life," "the American Dream," "rugged individualism," etc.

A wide variety of psychologists, sociologists, and educators have indicated consequences of maintaining the present system. While it certainly may be suggested that the system is functional and serves to produce a first-rate enterprise system, there are serious liabilities as well.[18] Many individuals and groups on the lower levels of the system may not rebel but may act in such a manner as to accept their positions; they accept the legitimacy of the system.[19] They develop excuses for not having attained higher positions when the whole society has told them in various ways that the field is open and they have been encouraged to rise. Guilt feelings must be directed toward objects other than that of the system or establishment, and in most cases the blame or cause for not having risen is directed toward the self. The individual may, therefore, attribute his lack of success to "bad luck," to scapegoats such as the Jews — a favorite theme of early Populist groups, to his own ineffectiveness or inattentiveness in school, to missed educational opportunities, etc. The school's function in this process is interesting. Students who will not advance in the social class system are told by guidance counselors, teachers, or school administrators that they have in some fashion been unable to match the requirements of the system. Different track systems (college preparatory, distributive education, general education, etc.) function in such a manner as to permit the separation of those destined for upward mobility and those who are to remain on the same level or move downwardly. Educators may attempt to minimize the psychological damage for many students by various counseling methods. However, in any final analysis, educators must directly or indirectly confirm the superiority of some and the inferiority of others, for some few will rise in the system and earn high rewards, and others will not. Such actions on the part of educators doubtlessly act in such a manner as to make the system of social class divisions functional. The toughest problem confronted by educators in such an effort is how to present relatively unequal goals with unequal rewards in such a manner as to make them appear equally attractive to all members of the student body.

Much controversy exists regarding the actual size and shape of the social class structure in the United States. Lloyd Warner and Richard Centers have both formulated concepts concerning the design of the social class structure.[20] Much of this work was done in the 1940s and 1950s. Critics have pointed out such work may now be outdated; they contend that the findings were biased in that they resulted from work done primarily with people in small towns and relatively closed communities where everyone was familiar with one another. Today, say such critics, we live in largely urban areas and have a highly mobile population who are not really acquainted with one another; and Warner's formulation of social class structure is dubious. Nonetheless, the formulations of Warner and others have tended to be widely accepted and often quoted.[21]

Warner's Theory of Social Class Structure

According to the research of Warner and his associates, the people of the United States can be divided into six social classes. These categories are as follows: (1) upper-upper class; (2) lower-upper class; (3) upper-middle class; (4) lower-middle class; (5) upper-lower class; and (6) lower-lower class.[22] Table I[23] indicates something of the relative size of these classes.

The upper-upper social class is composed of relatively few people. Individuals included in this group have long illustrious ancestry, great wealth, good education. They are white, largely Protestant in religious attitudes, and own great portions of the industrial wealth of the country. The lower-upper class is composed of a slightly larger group of people who have newly acquired wealth gained largely though industrial

TABLE I

RELATIVE SIZE OF SOCIAL CLASSES IN UNITED STATES BASED ON
FINDINGS OF LLOYD WARNER AND ASSOCIATES

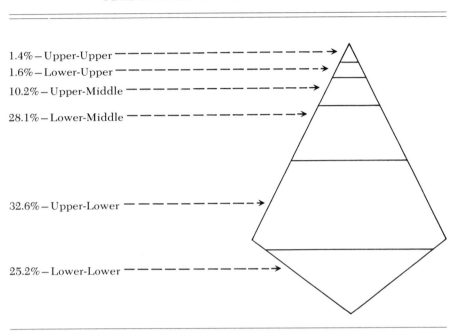

1.4% – Upper-Upper
1.6% – Lower-Upper
10.2% – Upper-Middle
28.1% – Lower-Middle

32.6% – Upper-Lower

25.2% – Lower-Lower

enterprise. They possess little in the way of distinguished family backgrounds. They are newcomers to their position in the social class system.
The upper-middle class is composed of the professionals such as doctors,
lawyers, and merchant chiefs. Occupational specialists have begun to
make up substantial portions of this class within the past 25 years. This
social class is frequently the highest social class present in small towns
and villages. Substantial portions of industrial management, industrial
technicians, and government experts belong to the upper-middle class.
The lower-middle class is made up of small merchants, the minor professionals such as teachers, preachers, and nurses. Small farmers belong
to this category. The upper-lower class is made up of large portions of
the skilled and unskilled workers. They affiliate with labor unions,
patriotic organizations, and the Democratic political party. They work
with their hands and are often called "hard-hats" or "blue-collar

workers." The lower-lower class is composed of those considered to be the "disadvantaged." They work, when they find employment, at janitorial services, domestic work, and menial tasks in general. A high rate of unemployment exists for members of this class. Many children in the lower-lower class are born out of wedlock and families are frequently on welfare. Many migrant laborers belong to this class.

In developing their formulations of the social class system in the United States, Warner and his associates relied heavily on objective criteria. While his methods have been much questioned by recent scholars, Warner suggested that social class membership could be measured by the Evaluated Participation (EP) and Index of Status Characteristics (ISC).[24] The former, the Evaluated Participation, is based upon class ratings by researchers familiar with the community and able to identify certain social interactions of the residents, such as club membership, church affiliation, and schools attended. The latter measure, Index of Status Characteristics, is based upon the socioeconomic characteristics of the residents of the community such as type of residence, dwelling areas, source of income, and occupation. The two measures combined are considered to provide reliable evidence on social class membership of individuals and groups.[25] An examination of the social classes in detail, as formulated by Warner and his associates, is of relevance to educators and composes a substantial body of materials of concern to sociology of education.

As the title indicates, the upper-upper class constitutes the highest social stratum in the United States. Warner estimated that the upper-upper along with the lower-upper combined to represent less than 5 percent of the total population.[26] Members of this class are characterized by the fact that they are very wealthy, have long and distinguished ancestry, are white, and are generally Protestant in their religious beliefs.[27] They tend to be of Anglo-Saxon extraction, and their families arrived at a very early date in colonial America. When reading history books, they are often studying incidents in which their own ancestral families were directly involved. Their homes, of which there are often several, represent cultural affluence and sophisticated taste. Within their homes there are frequently servants who have been with the family for some years. The children are often reared by trained nurses and governesses. Members of this class tend to practice relatively strict birth control, in order to prevent rapid division of their wealth.

The upper-upper class tends to be included in the "international set" and the "jet set." Children of the families will frequently receive substantial portions of their education abroad, preferably in Europe. Members of the upper-upper class are usually listed in such socially prestigious publications as the *Social Register*. They often have been reared in the glare of the public limelight and may develop tremendous ability to create a sense of ease and relaxation in their public relationships. This ability to act poised and polished may develop further into a charismatic quality and prove extremely effective as a political tool.

The families of the upper-upper social class often tend to be lineal in their value orientations, and an older matriarch or patriarch frequently plays a prominent part in the family decision-making processes. John P. Marquand graphically illustrated the lineal value orientation of this class in his novel *The Late George Apley*.[28] The more recent historical biography *Eleanor and Franklin*[29] suggests the dominance of Sara Delano Roosevelt in the lives of the thirty-second President and his First Lady. The struggle to be free of the authority figure in the family is frequently the theme of novels and biographies dealing with members of the upper-upper class. Value orientation in cultural attitudes and behavior of members of this class is a concern with the past. This concern with the preservation of the past is often manifested in the attitudes and behavior of its members.

The occupational choices of members of the upper-upper social class are indeed interesting. While they frequently own and control large industrial corporations, they often do not have sufficient interest or training to manage these industries. They may seek careers in politics by running for elective office, or filling positions as ambassadors abroad. Members of the upper-upper families, especially the women, seek outlets for their energies in philanthropic and charitable work. These families are often major financial contributors to many of the charitable institutions in the United States. They tend to have a recurrent problem of what to do with their time and energies. They often become patrons of artists and writers and sponsor them in their creativity. Members of the upper-upper class frequently serve as "financial angels" to institutions of higher education and are elected to boards of trustees, regents, and overseers at colleges and universities across the United States. They are often elected or appointed to positions of high public trust, since they are viewed as virtually incorruptible owing to their prior accumulation of personal wealth.

The children in the upper-upper class family are frequently reared by hired nurses and governesses and generally attend exclusive private elementary schools. These children are most likely to be "prepped" at well-to-do private secondary schools located on the eastern seaboard. Philips Exeter, Choate, Hill School, Phillips Academy, Kent, St. Pauls, and Groton are among the favorite institutions patronized by the upper-upper class families. After graduation from the private secondary schools, the men of these families are likely to attend one of the Ivy League schools such as Princeton, Brown, Harvard, Yale, Columbia, Dartmouth, or Pennsylvania, or one of the smaller but highly prestigious schools such as Williams, Amherst, or Bowdoin. The big three are considered to be Harvard, Yale, and Princeton. A father who is an alumnus of one of the above institutions will frequently register his son for admission to his university a few days after the birth of the boy. Women of the upper-upper social class may attend institutions of higher learning; however, it is not considered so essential for them to do so as for the men of the family. The upper-upper social class families prefer to send their daughters to one of the "Seven Sisters" such as Vassar, Radcliffe, Wellesley, Barnard, Smith, Mount Holyoke, etc. However, it is permissible for the women of this class to be educated abroad. In a pinch, however, they may attend an exclusive "finishing" school.

Attainment of an undergraduate degree usually concludes the educational careers of most members of the upper-upper social class. They do not feel the urgent need for higher degrees evidenced by the "perennial" student of middle-class origins. While the upper-upper social class members may continue their educations intermittently for some years, this process is largely informal and unsupervised, often taking the form of collecting artifacts of importance in anthropology, archeology, or forms of art. The individual's great wealth permits this. Often such persons become quite accomplished sportsmen and devote considerable time and effort to racing, polo, yachting, etc.

The lower-upper social class is composed of those individuals and groups who are usually considered to be the "new rich." Their families have generally acquired their wealth within the present or past generation. They are the newcomers to the upper class. Their wealth is based on industrial ownership. The lower-upper social class is not made up exclusively of those with WASP type characteristics but contains individuals and groups of almost any religious background and of any ethnic origin. There are blacks in the lower-upper class; however, they are relatively few in number and their wealth has largely been attained through interests in insurance and tobacco companies. There are many individuals of the Jewish faith included in the lower-upper class. Hollywood actors and actresses frequently achieve membership in the lower-upper class. Occasionally very well-paid athletes, who are able to hold onto their wealth, are considered to be in this social class.

Families representing the membership of the lower-upper social class include the Kennedys of Boston, the Rockefellers of New York, West Virginia, and Arkansas, the Fords, the Dodges, the Lyndon Johnsons, and the Lehmans of New York. Individuals often included in this social class are Frank Sinatra, Jack Nicklaus, Ronald Reagan, Howard Hughes, Aristotle Onassis, Bing Crosby, and Bob Hope. There is frequently a certain marginal quality characteristic of members of the lower-upper class. It is often assumed that these people display a certain insecurity which appears to be compensated for by much conspicuous consumption. This may be a form of adaptive behavior. At the turn of the century, Thorstein Veblen in his classic descriptions of the elite and their tremendous amount of conspicuous consumption appears to have been describing many elements present today in the behavior of the lower-upper social class.[30]

Unlike the upper-upper, members of the lower-upper are often the subject of gossip columns and grace the covers of slick-backed magazines. The contrast between the behavior and interests of Mrs. Eleanor Roosevelt and Mrs. Jacqueline Kennedy Onassis may be attributed in large part to differences in social class backgrounds and training. The upper-upper "arrived" a long time ago; not so for the lower-upper, who appear to feel that they frequently must "prove" their status.

The members of the lower-upper may be of any political affiliation; however, there is a tendency on their part to support the Republican party as best protectors of their financial interests. Those of the Roman Catholic and Jewish faiths compose substantial parts of this class; however, there is a tendency on the part of Protestants numbered among their ranks to identify with the Episcopal and Unitarian churches. As with the upper-upper classes, these families tend to be associated with large urban areas; few reside in small towns or villages. Thus, names such as that of the Kellys are closely associated with the Philadelphia area; that of the Johnsons with Austin; and the Kennedys with Boston. This is a reflection of the fact that their wealth is largely industrial in nature and urban based. It is also true that many of the lower-upper social class members have Northern origins, again reflecting the fact that their wealth is industrial in nature. They, with the upper-upper, may be considered the merchant princes of the Western world.

In terms of educational backgrounds and achievements, the lower-upper class members tend to model themselves closely upon the upper-upper. Frequently, the lower-upper social class family has contributed significant sums of money to colleges and universities. These gifts often assure the admission of future generations of the family to those schools or institutions of higher learning. Frequently, even the prestigious Ivy League institutions maintain admissions policies that recognize the gift-giving. Thus, one very prominent Ivy League college has seven categories by which a freshman may be admitted to the school. The first six categories pertain to various degrees of academic ability on the part of the applicant, and the seventh category is entitled "sons of friends of the university."

Children in the lower-upper class often receive intensive training in dancing, golf, tennis, ballet, yachting, sailing, etc., in order to prepare them for entering the social milieu. Great stress is placed on attending the "right" schools. It is essential to belong to the "right" clubs and associations such as the Junior League, Yacht Club, Athletic Club. Also of great importance is to have one's daughter invited to the correct debutante parties. A "coming out" party is a must. *The New York Times* and other eastern newspapers receive the engagement and wedding announcements of members of this class, and descriptions of such events are couched in overly modest terms rarely indicating the huge costs involved in the event.

The Kennedy family serves as an excellent example of the life-style maintained by the members of the lower-upper class. The sons of the family have been prepped at private nondenominational schools and most of the daughters have attended Catholic schools and colleges. At Harvard the late President John F. Kennedy served as chairman of the Frosh-Soph Party and threw a party in Memorial Hall still remembered by many. A Broadway musical show was flown in as part of the entertainment. Following his graduation from Harvard, he, at the insistence of his father, attended the London School of Economics, where he studied under the tutorship of Harold Laski, a prominent economist-sociologist. While members of the middle and lower class might opt to follow the same career pattern, few have the financial resources provided by a multimillionaire father to tide them over the difficult moments. Possibly, the informal education afforded the members of the upper class is more significant than the colleges and universities attended. Within the Kennedy family circle prominent actors, financiers, politicians, etc., were frequently dinner guests, and provided much cultural affluence for the Kennedy children.

The upper-middle social class constitutes the next social class in the system of stratification. At an earlier time the upper-middle class was composed almost exclusively of the professionals such as doctors, lawyers, and professors, businessmen, and large farmers and ranchers. Today, due to the great economic expansion that has taken place in the United States, other groups must also be included in this social class. The technical and clerical managers of giant corporations are now included. Added to this group is a whole array of individuals and families involved in the management of government agencies, medical institutions, educational institutions, economic agencies, etc.[31] In a very real sense a new upper-middle class has been developing over the past 25 years with the older values and principles of the independent professionals giving way and being superseded by those of the new corporate employee who manages much of the government and economy of the country. Still in many older and more rural areas of America, the old upper-middle-class occupations and prestige systems continue to exist, free from the incursions of the new managerial groups.

While the upper-middle class in large urban areas work in almost any section of the city, they tend to maintain residential homes in suburbia. They reside in the larger, more impressive homes of the community. A maid frequently works for the family on at least a one-day-per-week basis. While the upper-middle class plays a prominent role in the local or regional area, it rarely is visible to any appreciable extent on the national scene itself. It is often the highest social class present in the small towns and rural areas across the United States. The upper-middle class act as controllers of the government of their communities. They are elected to school board memberships and often hold such positions for years.[32] The upper-middle tends to preside over many aspects of local community life in the United States. Members of this class must usually be consulted regarding any changes to be made in the community, and their approval is mandatory prior to instituting reforms. Only after the members of the upper-middle have approved, will the reform usually be "sold" to the general public. Their professional and business positions are very respected by other members of the community, their opinion on a wide variety of community problems is considered important, and their agreement is seen as essential if the operation is to be successful. Thus, they are consulted when a new airport is contemplated, when a school is to be built, or when new streets are planned. It is usually estimated that the upper-middle comprises from 10 to 20 percent of the population of the United States. Their influence is somewhat disproportionate to their actual numbers.

The upper-middle social class is frequently portrayed in movies, TV, and the old-time soap operas. "The Edge of Night," "As the World Turns," and other modern daytime serials deal almost exclusively with families of the upper-middle social class. The high degree of prominence of the upper-middle is doubtlessly due in part to the fact that they virtually monopolize many of the highly specialized professions such as medicine, law, and banking. A great many people from all social classes must seek them out and secure their services. They touch the lives of many people. They are the record-keepers also in a very real sense; hence, they tend to be viewed by the general public as being experts in many areas other than those for which they have been trained. For example, some years ago when the federal legislature was in the process of holding hearings regarding needed educational reforms, few educators were called. But many bankers, doctors, lawyers, and businessmen testified before House and Senate committees on educational affairs.

The upper-middle class enjoys relatively high levels of economic security. The homes are often quite child-centered, with emphasis placed on the child's sustaining or extending the family's social position in the community or region. The child is expected to do well in school and to secure admission to a relatively prestigious college or university upon his completion of high school work. Little doubt is usually expressed by the parents as to the child's going on to obtain a college diploma and possibly higher degrees. The family often stresses the desirability of the child's obtaining a professional degree. They will frequently financially support the son or daughter's graduate education. Student marriages are a possibility, since the parental families can and are expected to aid the young couple. Great stress is generated when the son or daughter decides to leave school or to pursue a career or way of life not compatible with that planned by the parents.

The children and young adults of the upper-middle class are expected by their parents to achieve a high degree of social competence as well as academic knowledge with which to pursue their careers. The social graces are seen as vital to sustaining the family's status in the social stratification system. Thus, in colleges and universities, membership in nationally oriented sororities and fraternities is viewed with favor by the parents. The sons and daughters are often not so enthusiastic as are parents. In the South and Midwest, a son's initiation into Sigma Chi, Beta Theta Pi, or Phi Delta Theta will often be greeted with great family pride, as will also a daughter's initiation into Kappa Kappa Gamma, Kappa Alpha Theta, or Pi Beta Phi. Such social fraternity and sorority memberships serve as status symbols in the middle class. Academic honors are also considered desirable, and the Phi Beta Kappa key is smiled upon by members of the upper-middle class. They are very aware of its value on the job market.

Since many lower-upper social class families send their sons and daughters to private preparatory schools for their secondary education, it often occurs that the sons and daughters of the upper-middle class inherit the highest social positions available in the public secondary schools. Almost always, such youngsters are encouraged to enroll in the college preparatory type courses. As a result of coming from relatively culturally affluent homes, these youngsters do extremely well in the public schools. Studies reveal that either through ability, cultural affluence, or family status, they tend to monopolize the "A" and "B" level grades given by schoolteachers. Owing in part to the cultural nature of their home life, it is suggested by many sociologists and sociologists of education that large numbers of the sons and daughters of the upper-middle enter into careers involving the pure and mathematical sciences. They appear to have been exposed early to abstract and theoretical methods of thinking, whereas lower social class children frequently do not have such exposure. In short, the upper-middle-class children are early introduced to cognitive methods of study, whereas lower social class children are more aware of conative modes of learning.

While the upper-middle-class members are represented in all major colleges and universities, there is something of a tendency for the upper-middle class to prefer attendance at institutions such as Duke, Vanderbilt, Northwestern, Stanford, Columbia, etc. Such institutions usually rank among the first and second levels in the educational hierarchy. They are usually smaller than the large state institutions and somewhat more selective in their admissions policies. Many are private in nature. It is felt by the upper-middle-class families that such institutions can better customize their educational programs than the larger state institutions, but still provide higher quality programs than the many state and small private institutions.

Many members of the upper-middle class practice relatively rigid birth control; thus, they are able to concentrate their energies and financial resources on a few children. This assures them of great potential for social mobility. Frequently, members of the upper-middle are quite aware of their working class origins and ancestry. They may insist that a son get a job doing construction work for the summer or that a daughter "sling hash" in a resort hotel or restaurant during vacation. The money is not especially needed, but such experience is viewed as desirable in broadening social experience of the son or daughter. To further this experience, many colleges and universities attended by members of the upper-middle class offer the junior year abroad. The son or daughter thus lives with a family in Spain, Germany, France, or Italy for a year. In addition, families of the upper-middle class are often heavily involved in social or philanthropic work that brings them into close contact with the lower social classes.

Next in the social hierarchy we find the lower-middle class. The lower-middle class is generally viewed as the "backbone" of the small towns and rural communities across the nation. Great controversy exists over the actual size of this class. Most sociologists estimate that it composes from 25 to 35 percent of the total population. However, apparently many others also identify with the middle class. Surveys have shown that as much as 79 percent of the population consider themselves as middle class.[33] The lower-middle class hold a wide variety of occupations. The social class is composed of members of the lower level professions such as teachers, policemen, nurses, ministers, priests, etc. Other groups included in this class are small businessmen, small farmers, foremen, skilled laborers, clerical workers, and salesmen. Years ago this class was given the title "white collar workers" to separate it from the lower social class members who were called "blue collar workers." The titles are no longer appropriate with regard to shirt color, and there has tended to be a blurring of types of work that separate the two classes. The lower-middle class includes those people who have a limited but modestly adequate income and level of education. Salaries, while a factor in the membership in this social class, are a relatively minor factor, and general "life-style" of the individuals and groups is more important. The lower-middle social class is "family centered" and hence "child centered." The home is considered sacred, and emphasis is placed on the desirability of being respectable.

The lower-middle class is often viewed as the keeper of the values and mores of the American society. The new morality or emergent values have not met with great favor by many older members of the lower-middle class. It is not uncommon to hear older members of this class state their positions as "free born American citizens and taxpayers." They are the people of Main Street written about by many novelists. The lower-middle often have wide recognition throughout the local community. The individuals and families of this class often do the major share of work in the churches; they are "joiners" and the vital element in maintaining and managing many social, fraternal, and philanthropic agencies such as the Elks, the Moose, the Knights of Columbus, the Eastern Star, the Masonic Lodge, the VFW, the American Legion, the Four-H Club, the Y-Teens, the Girl and Boy Scouts, the Cub Scouts, etc. It is the members of this social class who are responsible for organizing church bazaars. They direct the activities of the PTA program next month. They are the people who collect for the United Fund, the Red Feather Drive, the Christmas Seal Drive, etc. It is through these and other organization memberships that many members of lower-middle class maintain the so-called "white power structure." Thus, a son who has become involved in some offense can usually be "gotten off" lightly through the contacts which the family maintains with judges, newspapermen, etc. Certainly, through such connections, the lower-middle families are able to keep the incident out of the papers.

The church plays an important role in the life-style of many members of the lower-middle class. The Methodist and Baptist churches often tend to represent the views of many of the Protestant groups in the lower-middle class. It is felt that regular church and Sunday school attendance is highly desirable and that religious training for the youngsters in the family is absolutely essential. The women of the families of the lower-middle may tend to be somewhat more regular in their church attendance than the men. The church is often closely affiliated with the business interests of the community. Thus, the women may cook the lunches for the Kiwanis and Rotary Clubs in the church basement, and the financial returns are donated to the church. Religiousness is often identified with "doing good deeds" by this class. The missionary zeal or evangelicalism of churches is identical in many respects with the cultural value orientation of the lower-middle class that stresses the doing value described in the previous chapter.

Other value orientations held by many members of the lower-middle class include great stress on individualism and future time. Children in lower-middle classes early are given tasks or chores that condition them toward assuming individual responsibility. Stress is placed on the future of the family, and as such the children are often afforded cultural opportunities and educational advantages not experienced by members of the lower social classes. The children of the lower-middle are often well prepared for entering school by their parents and other relatives. The grandmother in the family dares not come to the home for a visit without a few *Golden Books* or other childhood books in her luggage. Any adult relative will frequently be bombarded by the children of the family to read to them from books that they have already memorized verbatim. In short, many lower-middle-class children have, in reality, a half dozen informal teachers within their own families. They early acquire an appreciation of learning and internalize the importance of education. Respect for the school and teachers is inculcated prior to the actual attendance of the child in kindergarten or elementary school. Playing school is a favorite game of many lower-middle-class children. Their families encourage the boys of the family to play Little League baseball and other sports and view these activities as educational. Indeed, many young families travel widely and justify the trips and the expense as being educational and good for the children. Visits to Marineland, Yellowstone National Park, and Disneyland are considered to be educational experiences.

The lower-middle class may view religion as desirable, but they view education as absolutely essential. An old Southern minister once noted, "While God is revered, Education is worshipped." The statement is fairly accurate with respect to the lower-middle class. The teacher's goals and those of the lower-middle class have long been considered identical. Of course, the majority of teachers themselves belong to the lower-middle class. The lower-middle class family frequently expresses its willingness to "back the teacher up" in any disciplinary action he may take with respect to the son or daughter. Education is seen as a path for social mobility, and grades are indicative of the extent to which the child is capable of rising. Changes in grading systems are often fought by members of this class, who wish to have an understandable gauge of the mobility potential of the child. The lower-middle class is often highly social-class conscious and forbids its sons and daughters to play with or date youth from the wrong side of the tracks. Indeed, much of the charity work done by the lower-middle tends to function as an appeal to class consciousness. The child is urged to give his toys to those less fortunate or to poor children who "do not have a nice home as you do."

With respect to curricular matters, the lower-middle class often expresses the thought that education should be involved in moral training as well as in placing the traditional emphasis on the social and academic elements of learning. The educational system is expected to duplicate the family's efforts. Thus, the concept of the neighborhood school is important to the lower-middle class. It is seen as vital on the elementary school level and felt to be desirable, if possible, on the high school level. As the emergent value orientation has become more widely accepted among the lower-middle-class members, there has often been violent conflict with the other more traditionalist members of the lower-middle class concerning whether sex education should be taught in the public school system. Open discussion of sexual matters in the classroom is seen by many of the traditionalists as undesirable. Such families generally do not encourage such open conversations within the family. Many of the rules regarding attendance at school by pregnant girls or participation by married students in athletics are reflections of the lower-middle class's sense of morality and their power to impose it upon the educational system. Unwanted pregnancies are often a source of real trauma in the lower-middle class. A "shot-gun wedding" may be arranged with all the trappings of middle-class lace and formality, or the wedding date may be "altered" to afford the forthcoming child a reasonable chance of having been conceived in wedlock.

It is often suggested that a majority of public schoolteachers belong to the lower-middle class. They, therefore, tend to emphasize consciously or unconsciously the values, attitudes, and opinions of that class as the correct ones. They may use the middle-class values as a standard for measuring the performance of all students. Manners, tastes, behaviors, and dress held to be correct by the lower-middle class in the community may be upheld as the standard for all students. It is only within the past few years that this social class-centrism has been brought into the limelight as a viable standard for operation of schools. It is often suggested that teachers from the lower-middle class find themselves in opposition to children from the lower classes, and in turn, the children from the lower social classes feel the educational goals projected by the school by the agency of middle-class educators to be inappropriate or irrelevant for them.

As members of the community, teachers generally occupy an ambiguous position. They belong to few, if any, of the high-status organizations or agencies, such as the country club, the boards of trustees of institutions, or directorships in civic services. Like the minister or priest, they must often be conscious of the effect upon the community of their drinking publicly at a local bar or gambling at the local race track. It has been suggested that the older group of teachers in most communities have largely risen from the ranks of the upper-lower social class. As sons and daughters of day laborers and tenant farmers, they have tended to place great emphasis on the values of the lower-middle class to which they have risen. It may be that the emphasis on the virtues and values of the lower-middle class provides them a sense of security, having experienced the trauma involved in upward social mobility. Younger teachers doubtlessly represent an element born and reared in the middle class and consequently manifest a greater sense of security. Thus, they may more objectively view middle-class values and virtues and in so doing serve as more able educators for lower social class students.

Sons and daughters of most families in the lower-middle social class involve themselves in many extracurricular activities. Their families can easily afford the band instruments necessary. While part-time jobs are thought of as desirable by many of their families, they are not essential. Athletes in such families have freedom to participate in after-school sports. The lower-middle class children do very well on most objective type examinations. They have been conditioned in this effort as part of their home training. The language of tests and school texts is usually that of the lower-middle class. Large portions of the membership of school student councils, theater groups, and class officerships are made up of lower-middle-class students. The girls from this class may work in the principal's office during periods of the school day. Their families favor their children's participation in such activities, and school administrators often view such participation as supportive of their own efforts.

The upper-lower class comes next in the hierarchical arrangement. As with other social classes, disagreement exists concerning the proportion of the population that belongs to the upper-lower social class. It is usually assumed that between 25 and 35 percent of the people of the United States may be included in this class. They live in the respectable but less desirable sections of the city. In rural residences, they manage to keep the house painted, but it is less pretentious and lacks many of the luxuries taken for granted by the middle class. This social class is composed of unskilled workers within the industrial system. They are the renter-farmers, the lower-level civil servants such as street workers, garbage collectors, janitorial workers, and domestic servants. They are often viewed as "poor but honest" people by the higher social strata. They are considered "blue collar" workers in the older sociological terms. They work with their hands. Little mental skill is needed in their jobs. They often do routine work in their occupations. They tend in many respects to identify with the lower-middle class in their insistence on keeping their home areas clean and properly maintained. They view their jobs as a responsibility and attempt to be there regularly and on time. Many have no more than an eighth grade education. Few, if any, have attended a college or university.

As individuals, the upper-lower social class members are generally unknown to the larger community beyond the limits of their neighborhood blocks or rural roads. Indeed, many of the members of the upper lower class are referred to by the rest of the community not as individuals but rather in collateral terms as members of certain groups, gangs, or extended families. There is little "traffic" between the upper-lower class on a personal basis and members of the higher social classes. Modern media such as television and the movies have probably done more to remove the social isolation of this class than has the educational system. Much of their political power is exercised through collateral type organizations such as labor unions, church organizations, racial groupings (Sons and Daughters of Italy, Soul Brothers and Sisters, Irish Nationalists, etc.), and by ward bosses and block politicians. Generally, they have tended, in the past, to compose the "backbone" of the Democratic party. The failure of the Democratic party and its ward workers to secure a heavy turn-out of this social class on an election day spells probable defeat for that party. With regard to religion the upper-lower class tend to be included in all major faiths. However, their churches are often less luxurious, and their ministers, if Protestant, tend to be poorly paid and are often self-ordained. National Protestant denominations containing high percentages of the upper-lower class in their membership include The Church of the Nazarene, The Seventh Day Adventists, and minor branches of the Methodist and Baptist churches. Religious matters are frequently viewed as the domain of the women of the family, and adult males may attend only at necessary events such as weddings, funerals, and revival meetings. Often within the upper-lower families there is a sharp division of labor between men and women. Men often reject certain forms of household work as unsuitable for them and regard them as degrading or emasculating.

The upper-lower class tend to be more collateral in their value orientations than are the lower-middle, who place high esteem on individualism. The group is viewed as extremely important, whether it is the crowd who gather after work at the local tavern to talk baseball, football, politics, etc., or the group who compose the pool hall regulars. The same group affinity is observed within the structure of the neighborhood block. Thus, a Scotch-Irish, Polish, Italian, or Czech neighborhood may view the arrival of a black in its block with great resentment. Often blacks belonging to the upper-lower social class resent the intrusion of lower-lower-class blacks in their neighborhood and express the idea that such individuals and groups tend to "trash" the area and bring trouble with them in the form of police. Urban renewal often seems to have worked poorly because the program planners failed to consider the tremendous importance attached by the members of the upper-lower class to membership in stable and reliable groups, groups through which they find their own identity and power.

The upper-lower class do not enjoy great economic security. Their total wealth can be considered in terms of the job they hold, and a weekly paycheck is viewed as essential. Monthly salary checks place great burdens on these families. Often the type and make of automobile they possess is incongruent with their actual total income and general lifestyle. Savings are usually nonexistent, and in retirement they must depend upon Social Security or company pensions for their total support. They must often charge purchases, and making payments is a monthly ritual to be faced by many members of this class.

The upper-lower social class do not automatically reject the present system of education. Members of this class, along with many of the ethnic minorities which compose its membership, often express the wish that a son or daughter take advantage of opportunities offered by a good education. It may be suggested that one or more of the three "B's" are required by members of the upper-lower social class in order to attain success within the school systems. The three "B's" are brains, brawn, or beauty. The youngster with great academic ability will usually be spotted by the teachers and school administrators in the school system. This is especially true if the youngster attempts in any manner to emulate the behavior and attitudes of the middle-class educators. Frequently, such a youngster succeeds in obtaining a scholarship to a nursing school, an industrial training institution, or local college or university. The good athlete from the upper-lower class, who successfully rises out of that class via the sports world, is legendary. The girl or boy possessing great physical attractiveness may on occasion also be accepted by the middle class. Such an individual often acquires the status or prestige of the individual he or she is dating within the high school system. Thus, the banker's son may date the young lady from the wrong side of the tracks; however, she may be entertained more frequently at his home than he at hers. She tends to take on many of the social characteristics identified with his social class.

Few avenues for upward social mobility, other than that of formal education, are open to upper-lower-class members. The theater and certain areas of the sports world not requiring educational training or acquisition of cognitive type skills have long served as a vehicle for social mobility for members of this class. Examples of those who have used these pathways are Frank Sinatra, Marilyn Monroe, Perry Como, Rocky Marciano, Lawrence Welk, Clark Gable, and Mohammed Ali. The labor unions for some time also tended to function as a ladder system whereby young men of ability could rise in the system. Few even in the present period have completed more than a high school education, and often college or university work is taken at a much later time than is typical for members of the middle class.

Within the formal education system at both the elementary and secondary levels, the evidence suggests that while a majority of the "A" and "B" grades go to members of the middle class, the lower social class members tend to receive a major portion of the "C," "D," and "F" grades. It is questionable whether this results from a lack of appreciation on the part of the educators for the values and life-styles of the lower class students or whether the problem results from the cultural deprivation of the lower class homes. It is probably a result of both factors. Many present-day educators and behavioral scientists contend that the lack of academic success experienced by members of the lower class is suggestive of less preparation in early childhood for entering and competing in the middle-class-oriented schools. Head Start and Follow Through have been instituted as community programs designed to alleviate this lack of acculturation by encouraging culturally deprived students to attend these schools taught by educators trained to deal with lower class children. Such programs often begin for children at four years of age and may continue through the third grade. The results of these programs have not yet been fully analyzed. However, it is obvious that such federal programs are not intended to create two co-existing societies, one of middle-class groups and the other of lower class groups, but to create a ladder system by which individuals in the lower classes may achieve positions in society commensurate with their talents and skills. The programs attempt to create flexibility and viability in the older structure, not a new system of social stratification.

In the public schools, youth from upper-lower social class homes are frequently prejudged by the teachers. Educators attempt to make accurate judgments concerning the potential of such youth, and owing to the present size of schools and difficulty of becoming acquainted with these youngsters on a personal basis, often delineate career patterns for them in a wholesale fashion. The upper-lower are often urged to select occupational goals in distributive education, applied mechanics, home economics, and secretarial or clerical work. Such curricula obviously restrict their life-chances for obtaining higher status in the system, and to a degree this procedure tends to freeze them into the present status quo of society. The academic dropout rate is much higher among members of this social class than those of the middle or upper classes. Such failures often attribute their lack of success to "lack of interest," "not belonging," and "failure to get along with the teachers." Until recently, they were apt to accept the failure in some form of self-blame.

At the bottom of the social class system in the United States is the lower-lower class. Approximations vary greatly as to the size of this element of the population; however, most behavioral scientists estimate that 25 percent of the people of the United States may be included in this category. A substantial portion of non-white minority groups is felt to exist within the confines of this social class; however, substantial as these minorities are, the lower-lower class is still mainly composed of whites. Many of the whites making up this social class are descendants of early Anglo-Saxon settlers. They are typified by the residents of Appalachia, who have failed to improve their economic status over the years and have been bypassed by the economic progress of large groups of middle-class Americans. The lower-lower class is also composed of the second- and third-generation descendants of immigrants from eastern and southern Europe who have failed to rise in the system, as have many of their more fortunate cousins. It is composed of migratory workers, who travel with the vegetable and fruit crops from the Texas-Mexico border to Michigan in search of employment. Included in this classification are many non-white citizens. The American Indians on many reservations may appropriately be designated as members of this class, as may also black residents of urban ghettos and rural slums.

Irrespective of race and nationality, all lower-lower social class members have a relatively similar life-style, characterized by great economic need and little financial security in their lives. They reside in the least desirable areas. Many are functionally illiterate, and their schooling rarely continues past the eighth-grade level. The rate of crime among the members of the lower-lower social class is extremely high. Frequently such crimes are perpetrated on other members of the lower class. Crime and delinquency often become a way of life to some of this class and may be considered a sub-culture within the general society. Many sociological studies suggest that the more intelligent youngsters in the lower-lower class perceive crime as the only means by which they can improve their life-style. Often, especially in urban areas, prostitution, drug pushing, "the numbers racket," the bagman, the bookie, the skin game, flim-flam, the hustler, the pimp, etc., are regarded as facts of life by the lower-lower class, and children early become aware of these social phenomena.

Families of the lower-lower class have little recognition within the larger community, unless they are notorious. In fact, the community usually has difficulty in communicating with them, since the governing bodies rarely know with whom they should speak on behalf of the lower-lower class. Members of the class are rarely listened to. They are often viewed simply as recipients of surplus federal and state wealth in the form of welfare. Food stamps and the welfare worker are well known by this class. Their value orientations appear to be at variance with those held by the other social classes. They are strongly collateral; the group is all-important. And they are usually present-time oriented in their cultural values. There is a general assumption that this social class has not inculcated the work value or ethic to the same high degree as have the other social classes. However, such an assumption is doubtful. When employment is offered to members of this class, it is usually quite menial and carries a low salary. The women of this class usually find employment more readily than the men.

The family structure of the lower-lower social class is frequently highly fragmented, with children living with families to whom they are only indirectly related. The family unit is often highly unstable. This is notably true among blacks, and only to a slightly lesser degree true of whites. The family structural collapse for the blacks of this class appears to have begun in the slavery period, when owners frequently discouraged marriages among the slaves and broke up families for economic reasons.

Upon their emergence from forced servitude, many blacks found it difficult to reconstruct their family patterns. The Industrial Revolution
tended to lure many blacks from the rural slums of the South to the urban
ghettos of the North. The women often found their skills as domestics
more marketable than the abilities of the men. Hence, a matriarchal
structure in which the women were the dominant elements within the
family began to develop. Today, behavioral scientists often debate the
extent to which the economic system has emasculated the black man. It
is probably true for both whites and blacks in the lower-lower class that
the mother or grandmother in the family often represents the only form
of stability, affection, and interest that the individual is likely to experience in his or her early childhood. The male is often viewed as a rogue
from whom little is expected. Much of the burden of child-rearing lies
with the mother. Many of the women appear to be cyclic in their life patterns. Early unwanted pregnancy is followed by marriage, which in turn
is followed by a search for employment. The husband's desertion soon
follows, and the cycle repeats itself. An extremely high rate of illegitimate births exists in this social class.

Families in the lower-lower class are generally adult-centered rather
than child-centered. The child is frequently a helpful source of income,
especially among the migratory workers. The parents in the lower-lower
class do not closely supervise the recreation or entertainment of the children. Emotional control is not especially stressed, and children often
witness physical brutality in the family and in the ghettos or rural slums
in which they live. Due to limited economic resources and present time
value orientation, many individuals in the lower-lower class fall victim
to loan sharks. The pawn shop is a local institution within the ghetto.
Few in the lower-lower have an opportunity to rise socially or culturally,
save through some older established avenue such as the sports world,
the theater, organized crime, the music world, and gambling. While
many look forward to "striking it lucky," to the day when "my ship
comes in," or to some miracle, there is an increasing tendency on the
part of many of this social class in the ghettos to attempt to change things
themselves rather then rely heavily on fate or passiveness to obtain what
they view being enjoyed by the other social classes. As the late Adlai E.
Stevenson suggested, much of the world, and especially this class, is
part of the revolution of rising expectations.

In the schools, many lower-lower social class children feel that the
values being taught by the lower-middle social class teachers are

inappropriate and have little meaning. The families illustrated in the elementary texts have little in common with the families in the ghettos. The manners, behavior, and attitudes held to be appropriate by the middle-class teachers are not well understood by lower class children. Such things are not within their experience. Consequently, the children of the lower-lower social class are frequently early dropouts in the school systems. They tend to receive a large percentage of the failing grades given by teachers; they often find themselves in "trouble" with the teachers and school administrators. They often feel that the school counselors are more interested in gaining admission to good colleges and universities for middle-class students than in helping them in their problems with school work or with school personnel. When they "drop out" of school, they often join the permanent ranks of the have-nots within their ghettos and rural slums, for they will not have the social or academic skills requisite for social advancement in the industrial-technological system. The life story of the late Marilyn Monroe exemplifies the exception to the rule. Born in the lower-lower class, she rose to the lower-upper prior to her death. Her story of having been shifted from welfare home to welfare home throughout her childhood is commonplace among the lower class. An early marriage and divorce, again, are a typical pattern. She was able to rise only because of accidents. She just happened to catch the eye of movie producers and calendar watchers.

Citizens have viewed the dilemma of the lower-lower class with compassion and with demands that something be done to create a more viable situation. Federal programs such as Head Start, Follow Through, and schools for the retraining of dropouts have been instituted. However, they reach relatively few of those included in the lower-lower class. The federal and state governments have often attempted to organize some form of adult education for the unemployed. Welfare checks have sometimes been attached to programs in basic education. Programs instituted by minority groups such as the Blackstone Rangers and Black Muslims have possibly had more effect in creating an atmosphere conducive to educational progress than have the federal and state plans.

Centers' Theory of Social Class Structure

While Warner's theories of social class structure are generally accepted by sociologists of education, several behavioral scientists suggest that Warner's concepts of social class must be modified somewhat in order to be truly applicable. Many indicate that the six divisions created by Warner are unrealistic and that the categories should be collapsed to include only three major divisions: upper, middle, and lower. These same behavioral scientists feel that the entire concept is somewhat tenuous and that at best the people of the United States can only be classified into three relatively loose and overlapping categories. Other researchers have found that the size of the middle class is far larger than indicated by Warner and his associates.

Among those who have attempted to modify the theories of Warner, the work of Richard Centers appears to be worthy of consideration.[34] Centers, working from the point of view of a psychologist, suggests that subjective methods of measuring social class membership are more accurate than the objective methods used by Warner and his associates.[35] In short, he indicates that it is best to seek the individual's own estimation of the class to which he belongs. In his research, Centers asked individuals to what degree they felt they belonged to certain groups. A feeling of belongingness, a sense of identity, and a commonality of ideas, values, and beliefs with others of particular groups tended to indicate to Centers the social class membership of the individuals. He found that psychological "class consciousness" is the best indication of social class membership.[36] The term is not indicative of the "class consciousness" of the Marxist theorists who view the term as synonymous with "class conflict." Instead, Centers uses it merely to indicate the degree of closeness within the group rather than the distance between groups.

While Centers suggests that the individual may achieve this identity or "class consciousness" from the many groups that surround him in his daily life, the chief group from whom the individual takes his identity, and hence class membership, is the occupational group to which he belongs.[37] According to this theory, the individual in society comes to feel he belongs to his work group and accepts many of the same goals, values, and beliefs as his occupational peer group.

Centers asked the individuals included in his research either directly or indirectly to indicate to what class they perceived themselves as belonging.[38] The results of his study indicated that 3 percent felt they belonged to the upper class. Thirty-four percent felt that they belonged to the middle class. Fifty-one percent thought of themselves as being in the working class, and 1 percent indicated they were members of the lower class. One percent did not feel they belonged to any class.[39] Thus, Centers found that it was possible to collapse some of Warner's six class divisions and to add a new division which he labeled as the working class.

In short, it would appear that many individuals in the United States may, in a psychological sense, identify with the working class, but in terms of economic resources and educational attainment, belong to the lower classes. In other words, it may well be that if one applies objective measures, the structure of the social classes in the United States appears to simulate that of a pyramid with few at the apex and many at the base. If, however, one uses subjective methods for measuring the structure and asks individuals to indicate to which group they feel they belong then the resultant structure is diamond-shaped. In this latter instance, a much greater portion of the population would identify with the values of the middle grouping than would be true according to Warner's concept.

If one accepts the Centers theory of social class structure, there are several implications for education. First, it is suggested that teachers play upon and influence to a great degree the attitudes and class consciousness of other teachers. It would seem to imply that much of the life-style distinctive of teachers is perpetuated by the teachers themselves and can be modified to only a limited degree by outsiders. The occupational peer group becomes a mirror for the self. Thus, in a very real sense, if one accepts Centers' theory and its implications, in-service training and intensive group work of this sort not only tend to inform the teachers of particular approaches and methods of teaching but also tend to reinforce their attitudes and behaviors as members of the middle class. Since student groups resemble occupational groups to a large degree, one may rightfully raise the question as to the degree to which schools with homogeneous social class membership tend to reinforce class consciousness on the part of students or to produce a tendency in the social groups to overemphasize the class values of the social class present. To the contrary, to what degree is social class consciousness produced in schools with heterogeneous social class populations?

Leggett has also done substantial work in the area of social class identity, and some of his findings appear to raise questions as to the validity of the Centers theory.[40] First, it would appear from Leggett's research that the middle class does tend to gain much of its identity and class consciousness from contacts on the job and that the occupational peer group is extremely important and functions in this manner. However, the racial minorities appear in the same research findings to identify with ethnic colleagues, soul brothers and sisters, etc., far more than with their occupational peer group; hence, they find their social class identities through these ethnic groups.

Social Mobility and Education

There are various kinds of mobility or movement of a social nature in the class system of the United States. Usually, sociologists of education tend to mean vertical mobility or up-and-down movement in the social class scale when referring to social mobility; however, there can be horizontal mobility, in addition to other forms of social mobility. As has been indicated in the previous chapter, there is a value orientation within the major culture which suggests that all must strive for upward movement within the class structure. This is part of the Protestant Ethic or Mobility Ethic.[41] It is generally felt that upward vertical mobility is desirable. Thus, the farmer's son must simply not be a farmer and do what his father is doing, but it would be preferable for him to go on to the university and become a doctor or lawyer. The family would take much pride in this, as would his community. The garbage collector's daughter may attend nurses' school and become an RN; again, this would exemplify vertical upward mobility within the social class system. Any number of "rags to riches" stories could be recounted of individuals who have moved upward in the scale. The term vertical social mobility indicates to change one's position in the social class system either upwardly or downwardly.

Horizontal social mobility may simply imply that the individual or group has changed positions but remained on the same social class level. Thus, the principal of the high school shifts his occupational position to become a sales manager for a local Buick agency. He has probably only changed his occupation, not his social class standing. The school superintendent may accept a position as state supervisor of curricula. Chances are he has only changed his occupational position, not his social class membership. There tends to be much horizontal mobility in the American society; however, generally this type movement is not as highly prized as upward vertical mobility.[42]

Vertical mobility may occur between generations or in the same generation. If the mobility that has occurred has taken place between generations, that is, if for example, a son or daughter has risen higher or fallen lower than the father or mother in the social ladder system, we refer to this as intergenerational mobility.[43] To the contrary, where the mobility occurs in a single generation, that is to say, where a young man as a factory worker leaves that work and sets about opening a business for himself and succeeds in becoming a wealthy and independent businessman, we have what is called career mobility. There apparently tends to be slightly more upward vertical mobility in the society than downward vertical mobility.[44] Downward mobility is viewed as a rather disastrous thing in the society. It is often represented by the older, established family that once had money but through poor business transactions or other economically depressing factors tended to lose it. Such a family may maintain its life-style for some time; however, with the passing of time, it will become evident to the community that the particular family has lost its former position in the social class system and moved downward on the scale. This phenomenon is often the theme of many European novels.

Great argument has arisen among behavioral scientists as to whether we have maintained the amount of upward vertical mobility in the society today that existed in the past. Does the possibility exist today for a young man or woman to rise in the social class system to the same degree that it did two or three generations ago? Some behavioral scientists claim that the social class lines are hardening and there is much greater rigidity in the system.[45] Others argue to the contrary.[46] The question is a complex one, and most likely some elements of the population are presently afforded greater opportunity for upward social mobility than existed for them two or three generations ago. On the other hand, certain major groups may find it more difficult to move upwardly now than, let us say, at the turn of the century. The truth of the matter probably depends to a large extent on the section of the country in which one is living, the level of position from which one is starting, and the sex, race, and religious membership of the individual or group referred to.

Those who cite the belief that the social class system is becoming more rigid and that mobility is more difficult usually indicate, for example, that a young man could at the turn of the century begin work in the local bank as a janitor at fourteen years of age and, owing to the possibilities of upward mobility existent at the time, hope to proceed through the occupational ranks of the bank and end his career at sixty-five as its president. Today, they insist that this same type of mobility is very difficult and rare. They note that if one begins life as a janitor in the bank, he is most likely to end up at sixty-five as a janitor in the bank.

Furthermore, if one aspires to be president of the bank, his best opportunity would be to have been born son of the present president of the bank.

Several factors are generally thought of as contributing to the great social mobility of the past. These are immigration, industrialization, closing of the frontier, fertility rates of the various social classes, racial integration, etc. Briefly then, as millions of immigrants came to the United States after the 1850s and 1860s, they created a tremendous worker surplus. They filled the bottom levels of the occupations, thereby automatically raising almost all native-born Americans a step or two by virtue of the fact that a huge group had moved in to occupy a lower occupational level than they themselves held. While the European immigration has largely ceased, this same phenomenon occurs when Southern blacks or whites move to the Northern urban areas and fill equally low-ranking jobs in the cities. The original residents tend to be raised higher in the social stratification process. This also appears to occur when rural dwellers with few skills move into urban areas and are forced to take low-ranking jobs or remain unemployed. All others are automatically raised, since a new base has been created.[47]

Another factor contributing to social mobility within the social structure is the differential fertility of the various social classes. For many years, the upper-middle and upper social classes tended to have a relatively low birth rate. Consequently, as members of these classes died or departed from their jobs, replacements were needed. At the same time, the fertility rate among the lower social classes, as now, was comparatively high, and sons and daughters of farmers, factory workers, and unskilled laborers moved upward to fill these vacancies. Today, it is suggested that the fertility rate among the upper-middle and upper classes has increased dramatically; hence, the positions tend to go to the sons and daughters of these social classes, and few vacancies occur into which others can move via the social mobility process.[48] Another factor contributing to social mobility in the United States is the dropping of racial barriers that once forbade blacks and other non-white minority groups the right of access to certain jobs and occupations. While these barriers still exist to a certain degree, greater social mobility exists for this element of the population than in any earlier period. A third factor, of course, affecting social mobility is that of industrialization. The industrial process has produced technological change that has lowered the demand for unskilled labor and replaced it with a need for individuals with greater skills and knowledge. This industrial revolution has tended to create new and higher occupational positions into which much of the working population has poured. New occupational statuses or positions have been created with automation. Many suggest that as a result of industrialization and the creation of this vast body of new technical type jobs, the social class structure has been altered and is now diamond-shaped, with the greatest number of the population occupying the middle positions. The growth of industrial, educational, and governmental bureaucracies has also created a need for relatively great technological skills and has as a result doubtlessly brought about a need for more "white collar" workers and produced opportunities for social mobility for many.

While the above examples tend to signify the increase of opportunities for upward vertical mobility, such opportunities are most apt to be found for the "blue collar" workers to move into the "white collar" ranks. While this is certainly evidence of mobility, it is quite limited mobility. Many move, but few move very far within the system.[49] The young girl may take a course in secretarial work at her local high school. She then takes these technical skills to the large urban area and becomes a secretary in an industrial corporation. She has, indeed, moved upward on the mobility scale; however, the move has not been great or particularly dramatic. The young man may leave high school and go to work in a factory. He may not have a high school diploma. He may through his own ingenuity and ability become a line supervisor. However, here his upward vertical mobility usually ends, for he is confronted with the problem of education. His lack of a high school diploma or college and university training acts as a barrier, and he can advance no further. Past this point he must achieve the technical skills or knowledge felt to be essential from some type of educational institution or terminate his upward mobility.

The need for formal educational training has not always been so clearly a prerequisite for upward mobility. In an earlier period, many of the professions could be self-taught or knowledge sufficient for practice could be achieved by way of apprenticeship. An individual might become a medical doctor by trailing after a practicing physician and acquiring through practical experience the techniques and methods necessary in handling illness and health problems. Similarly, an Abraham Lincoln could privately read law and begin with his partner, Herndon, a law office in Springfield, Illinois, that would become the single largest in that city and receive one-third of the total legal practice of the entire area. Even after formal education was seen as necessary for certification for entering the professions, the amount of such education was often slight. Individuals from the lower classes could, for example, become certified teachers by scraping together a minimum amount of money and gaining relatively easy acceptance to a state normal for a period of six weeks to six months.

This situation no longer prevails; the apprenticeship and self-taught professionalism have entirely disappeared. Today, substantial financial investments are necessary to obtain a bachelor's degree, with its sometimes attached teacher's certificate. Admission to the medical and legal professions is still more costly. Even the profession of nursing is now in a somewhat confused state as a result of arguments over the desirability of converting the two- and three-year diploma programs into a degree program requiring more formalized educational experience of four years in length. Thus, slowly the drive on the part of the professions, as well as the requirements of the industrial-technological businesses, has produced a situation in which only those with great amounts of formal educational achievement may hope for entry and later advancement. In some respects the increase of formal educational requirements as a method of upgrading the competence of many professionals has acted to cut off entirely the opportunities for lower social class members to enter the professions and has resulted in a shutting of the door on upward social mobility for many individuals in these lower social classes. The lower social classes with their orientations of present-time value patterns and limited financial resources would appear to be increasingly frustrated in their efforts to gain upward mobility through entry into the professions or higher ranks of business and industry. The educational requirements have become increasingly "stiff." In the past generations, teaching and the ministry have tended to serve as "steppingstones" toward great social mobility for many families. The relatively easy admission to these two marginal professions by talented individuals from the lower classes permitted many families to rise in the social class scale.

The public secondary schools often act to minimize the potential social mobility of many minority students. Often students are confronted with a philosophy on the part of many teachers and counselors that emphasizes the desirability of their selecting occupational goals that insure immediate employment upon graduation and hence restrict great social mobility. Courses such as distributive education, applied mechanics, home economics, and secretarial and clerical skills are suggested as appropriate for these minority students. Such curricula obviously restrict their life-chances and tend to freeze them into a status-quo position.

Elementary and secondary schoolteachers and counselors act as "social elevator operators." They sort out the children with respect to those who have potential for great upward mobility, some mobility, no mobility, and those who are likely to be downwardly mobile. They place those with great potential for upward mobility in the college preparatory courses. Those who they feel have some potential mobility are placed in the general education courses, and those with little potential are admitted to courses in home economics, distributive education, etc. Finally, those who appear to have no potential for upward mobility will be placed in the "odd-ball" courses. Recent court decisions suggest that educators must now, more than ever before, scrutinize the moral and legal bases for assigning various students to certain educational "tracks." As has previously been noted, such action on the part of educators tends to make the social class structure and phenomenon of social mobility a functional reality.

CHAPTER 4

Concepts of Status and Role of Relevance to Education

The Perennial Problem: Defining Status and Role

In all societies at all times, certain basic functions must be performed if the society itself is to continue. These functions include such things as procreation, rearing and socializing children, providing defense, production and distribution of materials, in addition to food, etc. All population units, whether small groups or entire civilizations that spread across great continents, carry out these functions. They must organize to do so; otherwise, they would not be able to exist for any length of time. These functions may be broken down into divisions of labor or specific work positions. Those people occupying the positions are responsible for carrying out the basic and essential functions of the society. We have mothers, fathers, lawyers, soldiers, physicians, professors, policemen, teachers, etc. These social positions are referred to as statuses by sociologists of education and behavioral scientists generally. Usually, one occupies many statuses at the same time within a group or society.[1] Thus, he is a father, son, graduate student, teacher, member of the National Guard, etc., at one and the same time.

Much confusion exists with respect to the concept of status. The layman often refers to status as an evaluation. According to this definition, one has high or low status — meaning prestige or esteem. However, this is not the meaning of the term as used by sociologists of education and other behavioral scientists. Status to the social scientists means simply that the individual holds a position or positions within the social system.[2] The occupational position of educator, lawyer, physician, graduate student, garbage collector, etc., are all statuses in sociological terms. While each status or position has an evaluation attached to it by the general society, the esteem or prestige of the position is not to be confused with or used as a substitute for status. Thus, it may be said that generally the status position of teaching carries low prestige as compared with other status positions in the professional world.[3] On the other hand, most surveys indicate that the status of Supreme Court justice carries very high prestige. Status is simply a position in the group or society.[4] That position may be highly esteemed in some societies and lowly esteemed in others. In the older Oriental cultures the teacher-scholar status position carried the highest degree of prestige. In the Jewish community the status position of the educator is very high and is often superior in prestige to many other status positions within the culture. The term status does not in and of itself imply any particular value; it is simply a position in the social structure.[5]

Status positions are often divided into categories.[6] One may have a political status, economic status, religious status, recreational status, occupational status, educational status, etc. A man or woman may have certain positions in all of these categories or in any particular group of them.[7] An individual may be a Democrat, a property owner and taxpayer, a Methodist, a second baseman for the American Legion Club, a foreman at the factory, and a high school graduate all at the same time. Some behavioral scientists suggest that the individual's social class membership is the composite of all these statuses; however, as has been noted in the previous chapter, the writers and many others contend that a wider range of factors must be considered in determining social class membership.

Status symbols are the elements that indicate the nature of the office held by the man or woman.[8] These are the artifacts and symbols which go with the office or position that we have referred to as status. In an earlier period the Earl Marshal of England carried the mace before the king; the marshal rode a white charger and wore a jacket that resembled the king's personal hereditary flag. These were the symbols of his position or status. The President of the United States has symbols that surround his position as chief of state and head of government. The house he lives in is one of those symbols; so is the plane he flies in. All persons who fill certain status positions have status symbols. Today, the symbols often appear more conspicuous than the office itself. The man or woman who fills the position (status) often feels he must indicate in some manner or other the importance of his status position. He therefore surrounds himself with trappings — desks, nameplates, homes, or ritual, etc. — indicative of his status or position. Thus, the principal of the school may feel he needs a bathroom attached to his office. Since he holds a somewhat higher office in the educational hierarchy, the superintendent may feel that he must not only have a bathroom but also that it should be carpeted. The symbols of status need not be materialistic, although they quite frequently are. The actions of the teachers and others in permitting the superintendent to go first in line at the teacher's picnic is a symbol of status.

In an earlier period in the one-room schoolhouse, the teacher's symbols of status were the school bell, her gold watch, her charts, pictures, and materials, etc. Today, in a relatively urban type society, it appears that one is often not well known by many of the community members; therefore, one equips oneself with many signs and symbols that are meant to inform the uninformed as to the status one holds in society. All too frequently, the symbols become extremely elaborate and ritualistic.[9] The symbol rather than the status often appears to be what really counts. The student does the required work in order to wear or achieve the symbol. Undoubtedly the teenage culture tends to place great emphasis on the signs and symbols of status. Thus, we simply must have senior rings, caps and gowns, gifts at graduation time, National Honor Society pins, varsity athletic jackets, band uniforms, etc. One symbol of status is that involving the amount of space used for listing one's extracurricular activities in the class annual. The more activities listed and the greater amount of space consumed, the more obvious the importance of the statuses the individual holds in the eyes of his peer group. Again, emphasis on the signs and symbols often tends to obscure the actual status position and the functional importance of that position in the school's affairs. Individuals in the highly competitive society we live in often feel that the symbols must be used to support the status position rather than the status position merely being indicated by the symbols and signs.

Status positions change slowly within a society.[10] Thus, if Bill Thornton leaves a principalship in the school system, the principalship remains largely unchanged. Richard Horn simply comes in and fills the position (status). Should he, in turn, change jobs, the position of principal continues to exist. There is a basic need for the position or status in the society, and it is possible for that status to change only slowly.[11] If we could bring back a physician from ancient Egypt he would recognize rather quickly and feel kinship with the modern neuro-surgeon. Six thousand years have gone by, and the status position in society for dealing with illness still continues to be essential. Status positions are somewhat detached from individuals and are thought of as being depersonalized.[12] One frequently hears the expressions, "Don't kill yourself at that job; it will still be around when you and I are dead and gone"; "You are not indispensable; someone else will come along and do the job when you leave it"; or "Don't worry, leave the problems of the job on the shelf when you leave the office . . . don't take your occupational troubles home." Such expressions indicate an awareness on the part of individuals that they can detach themselves from the position or status and that it can be depersonalized.

Role Expectations, Consensus, and Conflict and Education

The concept of role suggests that while certain methods of carrying out the duties of the position are imposed by others surrounding the man or woman holding the status position, there is additionally the potential for individualized interpretations of the way the position should be handled.[13] Role behavior involves the personal and individual element as well as sets of traditional expectations that surround the duties of the position. Thus, the person who becomes a teacher occupies a particular status in the society. The members of the community, other teachers, principals, students, etc., hold certain expectations of what the teacher will do—how he or she will carry out the duties of the status. The occupant of the position, the teacher herself, probably accepts many of the public's dicta on teacher behavior and carries them out as part of the job; however, the teacher may also add a personal element or individualized interpretation in his or her job which is unique and unlike the behavior of other teachers. One teacher always makes a point of smiling at her students as they enter the room and attempts to say something pleasant to each of them. Another teacher attempts to set an extremely serious atmosphere and uses a "no-nonsense approach" from the moment her class assembles. Thus, individuals occupying a teaching position (status) in the society often interpret or act out the role in some aspects that are quite similar, and in addition, give the role certain individualized interpretations that make that particular teacher very different from others. The individualized interpretations given the role may result from differences in social background, teacher-training programs attended, different family structures, different educational experiences, different cultural values, social class membership, etc.

The group or society works and is productive because it is possible
to achieve a cohesiveness through a common understanding as to what
each position (status) is intended to do and generally how the role behavior attached to the position is supposed to be carried out.[14] There is,
of course, some margin for individuality permitted in carrying out the
role. Most sociologists consider role to be the dynamic element of society that makes it possible for people to work together and carry out
various tasks.[15] While mores and norms are broad expectations of how
people should act, status and role imply much more specific expectations. Since all people in the group or society occupy many statuses, each
individual has a rather specific understanding of what is expected of him
and what he, in turn, may expect from others. The process is reciprocal.[16]
A principal holds certain role expectations for his teachers; and they, in
turn, hold certain role expectations for him. If both sets of role expectations are relatively similar and mutually agreeable, it is usually theorized
that the organization will likely be cohesive and highly productive.

All positions in a society are linked together in a close-knit relationship and are dependent to a high degree upon one another. Similarly,
the persons occupying the positions can work together because they have
a common set of expectations as to each others' behavior in these positions.[17] The students usually know in a general way what to expect from
a counselor, from a dean of men or women, etc. The principal and superintendent have a common set of expectations as to each other's role
behavior. The chairman of the academic department holds sets of role
expectations for the departmental members; and they, in turn, hold
expectations for the chairman. Status and role cannot exist outside of a
group context. Robinson Crusoe needed his man Friday in order to create
status positions and role behavior.[18]

Where disagreement or lack of understanding exists as to the correct
role behavior for the position, sociologists of education refer to the condition as role conflict, role strain, or role stress.[19] Thus, we find ourselves
in role conflict when our behavior in a particular status does not conform
to what others in surrounding positions feel we should be doing. Some
years ago, the wife of a public school secondary principal in New England decided on a writing career. She authored the novel *Peyton Place*.[20]
The community residents appeared to disagree with her role behavior in
this effort and the condition of role conflict arose. A teacher entering a
new job may occasionally find that the role expectations held for him or
her by those surrounding him do not conform to the expectations held

by the teacher himself. The other teachers and principal may, for example, be members of the "old guard." They may view the teacher's role as being basically conservative, oriented toward maintenance of good discipline, use of much rote memory, and great structuring of learning situations. To the contrary, the new teacher may view the role of teacher as being concerned with and involved in giving the children a sense of self-confidence, creating conditions for cooperative behavior among students, instilling a love of school in the class members, and in general working through a rather loosely structured learning situation. These two sets of role expectations, if perceived by both the other teachers and the new teacher, are likely to result in conditions of role conflict among the teachers.[21]

Another example of role conflict or role strain is evidenced in the familiar story of the coach or teacher who has been so successful in the role interpretation attached to his position that he is offered a more financially rewarding status position in the system as assistant superintendent. Having entered the second position or status, he may discover that new sets of role expectations are held for him in his new position. Even his old friends, students, and buddies appear to hold new sets of roles appropriate for him in his new position. They don't treat him as they formerly did. His status has changed, and they have taken this into account in their own role behaviors. The old role behavior that he formerly had is no longer appropriate. His wife's status has also changed, in that her husband has a new position; consequently, she may find that the method of acting as coach's wife is no longer suitable and that she must shift radically in the discretion of her conversation, treatment of old friends and intimates, drinking habits, etc. After a few years, the new role adjustment may take place, or such individuals may continually express regret in surrendering the former positions and the comfortable roles attached to the statuses.

Another form or type of role conflict is evidenced in situations in which the individual has many statuses. As a holder of many positions, he may find that certain behavior appropriate in carrying out one particular status is unsuitable behavior in carrying out another status.[22] An individual teacher may be commander of the American Legion local post, a tenured teacher, and a coach in the public school system, all at the same time. His buddies at the Legion Club expect him, in his role as commander, to throw a really good "beer blast" and to live it up with the boys. As a secondary schoolteacher and coach, the principal and superintendent expect him to conduct himself as a model of behavior suitable for the students and athletes. If the teacher perceives the differences in role expectations, he is faced with problems of what to do. In such conditions of role conflict, the individual may seek solutions of various sorts. He may attempt to "block" his mind and ignore certain of the role demands. He may attempt to keep the roles quite separate. Thus, he acts differently in each case. He may engage in the drinking and "fun" while at the Legion Club and act in quite a different manner while with the students and varsity athletes. The conflict, if he recognizes it, may create personal psychological problems for him and interfere with all aspects of his behavior. He may act in a highly selective manner and accept the roles he likes and reject the roles he does not like. Thus, he may simply stop going to the Legion Club or give up the coaching position. He may use substitute personnel and have them carry out the duties attached to certain of his roles. In this instance, the teacher as Legion commander may assign the duty of organizing the "beer blast" to others. The superintendent of schools may, as an example of this solution to role conflict, have secretaries or assistant superintendents perform on a temporary basis particular duties attached to the superintendent's own role that he does not wish to carry out himself. Thus, the secretary or other personnel must explain to the irate parent the reasons for their son's expulsion from school or tell the disgruntled businessmen that the superintendent is heavily "booked up" this afternoon and is scheduling no new appointments. The assistant or secretary can then proclaim her own lack of further information upon demands by the parents or businessman as to other courses of action. In one manner or another, all individuals attempt to reduce the role strain or role conflict involved in their status positions.[23]

The married woman teacher with children possibly may also find herself in various forms of role conflict. As mother, teacher, wife, daughter, DAR member, neighbor, etc., she may find that she is subjected to relatively different sets of expectations in each of these individual roles. She may find that she is unable to comply with or give sufficient time to one of several roles, owing to demands for time in other roles. Or she may find that she is carrying over role behavior in one role to another where the situation is inappropriate. Thus, she talks to her husband at the breakfast table in an almost identical manner to that in which she would use with her class. Sociologists and sociologists of education usually refer to this transference of inappropriate role behavior as role discontinuity. Possibly, the female element of the population is more subjected to role strain than are males. This is especially true for those who attempt both marriage and careers. They possess many statuses and great variation in the role behavior is demanded in each of these positions. Robert K. Merton has defined the condition of possessing many different roles as a result of occupying different statuses as role-set.[24] Role-set is a group of different and distinct statuses occupied by a single individual.[25] Should the above female teacher obtain a divorce, then her role-set or particular group of statuses changes at that point. A particular role-set exists only at one specific time. As the statuses change so does the role-set.

Role Internalization and Education

Behavioral scientists who work in role theory often suggest that social roles are the elements in society that directly link the social structure to the individual's personality formation.[26] According to such concepts, the individual tends to internalize, as part of his self-identity, many aspects of the role behavior required in the status or position both before and after he has entered the position itself. Thus, the young premedical student is forced to work long and difficult hours at his studies. It is often theorized that he will internalize this behavior and perseverence and as a physician conduct his role in a similar manner. As a physician it is hoped that he has internalized much of the student training role and that a mode of behavior appropriate to the scientific laboratory will become part of his personality by the time he has become a medical doctor. In this effort, he will, as a physician, display little emotion or personal feeling. The Ph.D. candidate may feel that he is being bruised and battered by a group of disagreeable professors. Basically, his adaptation of a "tough skin" mode of behavior in the role of graduate student is expected to be internalized so that, in his later position as professor himself, he will disregard much of the personal behavior of his colleagues and view them in an objective and detached manner. Thus, the individual's personality needs and the demands of the status position tend to become compatible.

Several systems have been established of both a formal and informal nature for inculcating correct role behavior in teachers and educators. The first one is the formalized training instituted at schools of education and teachers' colleges. The student-teacher studies various role interpretations of methods in which the position of teacher should be handled. Often, however, the newly certified teacher discovers that the role interpretations posed in the teacher-training programs are not the same ones held to be correct in the community where the new teacher has been hired. Often the new teacher notes that the teacher-training program taught him nothing and that much of the material was inappropriate. Such teacher-training programs often do not take into account the relatively different role expectations held for teachers in different types of communities. The training programs often create a role interpretation for the position of teaching that does not exist in the actual situation. The model behavior proposed in teacher training institutions is often uni-dimensional; whereas dozens of such interpretations or sets of expectations exist, depending on the type of school and the area in which it is located. Occasionally, the newly certified teacher finds total incongruence between the role interpretations taught to him at the school of education or teachers' college and what is expected of him on the actual job.

Informally, the teacher may have achieved a set of role expectations for the position long before he or she has actually entered the position (status). The child may observe the teacher and be tremendously impressed with the educator's authority and splendid personality. When the child or adolescent matures and becomes a teacher in his own right, he may disregard much of the material taught to him in his teacher-preparation program and revert to the role interpretations evidenced by his own earlier teacher or teachers. Conversely, the new teacher may interpret his role as teacher in a manner very opposite from that displayed by teachers under whom he has studied. Thus, we may have, according to sociologists in education, positive or negative role models from whom the new teacher learns his role behavior as educator. A wide range of such positive or negative role models appears to be available to him on an informal basis. Teachers' colleges and schools of education rarely appear to take this possibility into consideration. Table I indicates the type of role models followed by 142 "Teachers of the Year" in a study conducted by the writers.[27] The teachers had been named as Teacher of the Year from their respective states within the past five-year period. No more than three teachers were from a single state. In the questionnaire, these high-quality teachers were asked to identify, if possible, the status of individuals whom they most imitated in their own classroom teaching methods and techniques.

TABLE I

ROLE MODEL SELECTION OF 142 "TEACHERS OF THE YEAR"

Role Model Status	First Choice	Second Choice	Third Choice	Total
My own elementary teacher(s)	23	9	8	40
My own junior high teacher(s)	3	9	1	13
My own high school teacher(s)	48	24	35	107
My undergraduate academic prof(s)	20	24	5	49
My graduate academic prof(s)	12	28	22	62
My education prof(s)	5	4	7	16
Teacher or prof(s) under whom I did student teaching	12	8	11	31
Another teacher alongside whom I have taught	18	30	35	83
Other	1	2	8	11
None	--	4	10	14
Totals	142	142	142	426

The above study of utilization of role models by high-quality teachers suggests that 38 percent of the teachers in the investigation attributed this function to their own elementary and secondary school teachers. Twenty-six percent viewed their academic subject-area professors as their chief role models in teaching. Only 11 percent attributed this important function to their education professors or personnel in charge of student teaching. The data seems to indicate, certainly for teachers of the above type, that institutional programming of role models into teacher-training operations appears to come too late or is insufficient to have great effect.[28]

Many behavioral scientists suggest that role inculcation takes place to a large degree after the individual has entered the position (status). Therefore, a thorough program of in-service training might well include the study of aspects of role behavior, as well as knowledge of skills and methods in teaching. The informal atmosphere of the teacher's lounge may act in such a manner as to permit the various schools of thought, role interpretations, to be brought into competition with one another. Thus, the "iron guard" may insist in conversation that students be "shaped up." The young or old liberals may have their say on what is the correct role interpretation for teachers, etc. The beginning teacher who finds the role expectations of a majority of teachers in the building incongruent with his own interpretation may, after several years, find that his own role interpretation has shifted sufficiently to make possible a cohesive and workable relationship between him and other teachers; or he may find that other teachers have shifted sufficiently in their role interpretations to accommodate his views.

The condition in which there is a great amount of mutual agreement as to the interpretations of how one should carry out the role of being teacher, superintendent, student, counselor, etc., is referred to by sociologists of education as role consensus. The sameness of role expectations or role consensus appears to be vital and essential for the creation of truly workable and productive organizations. However, the achievement of role consensus is not easily reached in a highly sophisticated and complex society.[29] The sheer size of the public schools, along with the diversity of backgrounds from which the educators and students come, makes such a task increasingly difficult. When the schools were more decentralized in an earlier period, consensus of the group working in a particular small school was more easily achieved. Once the students were placed in one, two, or three giant schools where great differences exist in social class origins, ethnic backgrounds, etc., role consensus is extremely difficult to find. Possibly this may be one of the main reasons why such emphasis has been placed in recent years upon the importance of communications among dissident groups. An understanding of the differential role expectations may be produced through various methods, whether they be free exchange of ideas, sensitivity sessions, arbitration, etc. Often when a great variety of role expectations and interpretations exist which are at great variance with one another, it appears that the organization is "coming apart at the seams." Such situations are often apt to catch the public's attention in the news, since it implies that a crisis condition exists.

Conversely, we often find teaching situations in which the individuals appear to be perfectly adapted. Where there is consensus as to the role of the teacher among the teacher colleagues, principal, students, school administrators, and general community and by the teacher occupying the specific position, we may witness the rather delightful harmony expressed by those around the teacher who often refer to him as "a born teacher" or "a natural teacher." Frequently, this simply means that the individual teacher referred to has probably found it possible to accept the role interpretations or expectations of others who surround him and has added a special and unique quality to the role that is his own. The high dropout rate of beginning teachers probably reflects a failure on the part of the individual and teacher-training institutions to properly interpret the role expectations desired on the part of the local community for those who are to fill the teaching positions.

Ascribed and Achieved Status and Education

Two types of statuses are of concern to educators. These are achieved and ascribed.[30] The ascribed statuses are those positions that do not rely or depend upon the individual's abilities, skills, or talents. Being born a male is an ascribed status.[31] A female at birth also has a distinct ascribed status in the society, as every member of the women's liberation groups will tell you. Certain rights, duties, and behaviors are permitted as a result of ascribed status positions one holds. Limitations are often placed on the behavior of those in ascribed status positions. In our society, a young man or woman may receive a driver's license at sixteen years of age. The society ascribes to them the status of adults at this time with respect to having the rights to drive automobiles. Similarly, the society ascribes the status of legal adults to them at eighteen years of age by giving them the right to vote. A man is considered ready for retirement and must usually leave his job at age sixty-five. The society gives him the ascribed status of old man and regards him as such, irrespective of whether he is able or not. Social norms appear to designate many of the ascribed statuses in any given society.[32] The Pepsi song indicating that age is not a factor in the society—and hence, that ascribed statuses based on age have been abolished—appears to have had little effect in most cultural areas. One does not expect a six-year-old child to act as an adult or to run for the United States Senate. We have given him an ascribed status position and expect all elements of the population to react to him in accord with his ascribed status.[33] The eighty-year-old, irrespective of his physical prowess, is not expected to turn out for professional football practice. The society does not ascribe that status as suitable for him. It does not permit him to compete. Nor does it usually allow women to enter the professional football game as competitors, although there are a few exceptions. Again, the society ascribes this status only to males in certain age groups. In short, ascribed status is indicative of a relatively fixed way of determining the divisions of labor.

Achieved status means that the individual or group has struggled in some manner or other to acquire the position. Achieved statuses are left open to be filled by individuals who can successfully compete for them. Being a male is not an achieved status; one is a male because one is born to that condition. He is given the ascribed status of male in society with the special rights and duties connected to that sex role. Becoming a teacher is an achieved status. It is not a predetermined condition. Becoming a school counselor is an achieved status; the individual becomes one through his efforts. Some societies have large numbers of ascribed statuses. Others, such as ours, take great pride in the large number of achieved statuses they possess.

Examples of societies possessing great numbers of ascribed statuses are those of the primitive tribes and feudal kingdoms. In ancient Egypt almost all ranks or positions were ascribed and had prescribed sets of role behavior attached to them. Therefore, education consisted largely of training suitable for occupancy in a preordained position. One had little or no choice. Pharaoh must occupy the throne; he could not abdicate or retire as private citizen to the countryside. He was the reincarnation of Amon-Ra, the sun god, and had no choice in the matter. One pharaoh, Ikhnaton, did attempt to deny this ascribed status, and civil war immediately erupted. Pharaoh automatically married all of his sisters. These women had no choice in the matter; their status was ascribed from the moment of their birth. One such female would sit on the throne beside pharaoh as his sister-queen. Her behavior in that role would be highly prescribed, and her freedom of choice either in her status or role would be largely nonexistent. Selection of pharaoh had little to do with intelligence or ability. Usually he was simply the previous pharaoh's eldest surviving son.

During the feudalistic period of western European history, positions, although somewhat less deified, were equally ascribed. The positions of serf, yeoman, knight, artisan, etc., were fixed, and one's status position was determined at birth. Irrespective of intelligence or abilities, it was extremely difficult to change one's position or compete for another status. The eldest surviving son of the monarch, were he born in wedlock, would succeed to the throne. Intelligence and abilities had nothing to do with it. An actual idiot did succeed to the throne of Spain. King Carlos was an imbecile, and King Philip of Spain, seeing that the ascribed position of monarch would fall to his eldest son who just happened to be a raving, homicidal maniac, was forced to have the boy put to death. He would otherwise have inherited the throne with no questions asked. Achieved status became something of a possibility in the Italian Renaissance period, and achieved status became a relatively common thing in Tudor England under that family of monarchs. Sons of butchers, merchants, and yeoman farmers became counselors of state under Henry VII, Henry VIII, and Elizabeth I. Such a policy of permitting many to compete for the highest positions in the kingdom may be attributed to the wisdom of these rulers or it may have become a necessity owing to the fact that the nobility had slaughtered one another in the War of the Roses.

All individuals in our society have some statuses which are achieved and some which are ascribed. In the United States it is felt desirable to keep the ascribed ones to a minimum. However, all societies do have some ascribed statuses for the people. Thus, all differentiate on the basis of age and sex. Babies, young children, youth, young adults, etc., have ascribed status within the culture. Ascribed status permits greater security within a society. There is less competition for everyone. Not all positions are "up for grabs." Such societies appear to have a more relaxed atmosphere about them. On the other hand, in societies in which there are many achieved statuses, or where in a theoretical manner all positions would be "on the line," we may expect to find great amounts of social tension and much anxiety. A society with many achieved statuses is likely to be a very dynamic society, but not always a very happy or contented one. Much of the executive organizational structure of the business world is presently based on high percentages of achieved statuses. We may, therefore, witness something of the "dog-eat-dog" atmosphere existent in the higher levels of such organizations. One dare not relax because someone else will get his job. It is a very competitive world.

The more industrialized a society is, the more specialized the divisions of labor are bound to become, and in such a structural situation, the number of achieved statuses tends to increase enormously. In an industrial-technological society, new positions are created which have not previously existed. There are few rules to govern who shall fill these statuses. There is a tendency to leave them open and permit them to be filled by competition. In primitive or feudalistic societies, change is very slow; few new positions are created and gradually those which do exist tend to acquire rules and regulations which eventually convert them into ascribed positions. As a carry-over from these societies, most groups today consider sex to carry with it an ascribed status. Thus, males in an earlier period received one type of education and females quite another. Martin Luther appears to have agreed with the desirability of a different type of education for boys and girls. Historically, one pattern appears to emerge: as societies become more technologically oriented, there is a marked tendency to shift from ascribed status and roles to achieved status and roles. Today, many women's liberation groups in their programs and political declarations are advocating a further increase in achieved statuses and the demolition of many of the ascribed statuses. Such action represents a process which is already underway in most industrialized nations. The elimination of race and ethnic origins as ascribed statuses is still another example of this process.

Where many ascribed statuses exist, the educational goals and aims may be clearly defined and nothing other than preparing individuals for the preordained statuses which they will later occupy in the society need be done. The blacks for many years were considered suitable for only certain menial tasks; therefore, their educations were often of only the most simplistic nature. While there were certainly prejudices involved and much wrong was done, the fact that the black existed in an ascribed status and could not compete for other jobs outside those included in the ascribed status areas was functionally related to the types and levels of education given him. The whole situation was morally and ethically wrong, but it was functionally correct. It worked all too well. The conflict between the educational philosophies espoused by Booker T. Washington and W. E. B. DuBois appears, upon examination by sociologists of education, to be a conflict between partial acceptance of ascribed statuses by Washington and rejection of this whole thought by DuBois, who opted for achieved status.

Where large numbers of achieved statuses exist, the educational systems and educational personnel are confronted with a very difficult set of tasks. As has been noted, such situations are characterized by great anxiety and tension. Many statuses are those "on the line." They are "up for grabs." Educators must, to a degree, gamble on the potential success of particular students and plan, if possible, for alternate statuses into which the individual can fit. Nothing appears to be a certainty. Thus, the educational programs are created with dual majors, majors and minors, second and third areas of certification, situations in which lower academic degrees may differ from more advanced degree areas, etc. Such programs must be extremely flexible and conducive to rapid change. Undeclared majors in college must be permitted to exist so that the student can, at the last possible moment, shift into possible status positions that have developed or opened. In situations in which many achieved positions exist, counselors and other educators are presented with an immeasurably more difficult job than where the achieved statuses are relatively few. Our educational system must permit "late bloomers" a second or third chance to come back into the school system to prepare for a different status position than that which they originally stated in their educational plans. In a society with great numbers of achieved status, the educational system often resembles nothing so much as "organized chaos." Often this havoc is seen as bad and detrimental to the school organization. Actually, such difficulties are probably very predictable and necessary, in view of the increase in achieved statuses currently evidenced in the society.

Concepts of Teacher Status and Role

While the teacher has a particular status position in the general society, teachers have several other social relationships which are closely tied to and part of that position. For example, the status of elementary and secondary teachers frequently involves his or her acting in the capacity of classroom teacher, disciplinarian, community worker, adviser to students, evaluator, etc. Robert K. Merton has referred to these multi-roles as role-set.[34] Thus, the university professor in his position is more than just a professor; he is involved in the social acts of being a researcher, student counselor, clerical worker, classroom teacher, and committee member, as a part of his overall status of college professor. According to Merton, a role-set is a complex package of roles that center on a particular social status.[35] Other social scientists attach other labels to these relationships. It may be assumed that teachers do not give equal attention to all of their roles. They may emphasize one role and neglect another. We generally do not view with equal pleasure all the aspects of our job; hence, there exists a great deal of individuality in the areas of the job we emphasize. It is probably this individual selection of roles to be emphasized which tends to create variety in the behavior of individuals who fill the teaching position. Such flexibility satisfies the individual's personality needs and the organizational demands. The ability to specialize in certain roles makes it possible for a great many different people to fill the same status position.

To use the well understood status position of housewife as an example may add clarity to the concept of role specialization.[36] While all housewives, to a degree, engage in the same roles included in carrying out the position, they may differentiate as to the degree they fulfill any one of these roles. One housewife may love to cook. She views this as the mark of a really good housewife and works in her kitchen at this task constantly. She may do only a minimum amount of work in the other roles attached to the position. Another housewife may feel that a clean and tidy house is the requisite of the position and spend a great amount of time achieving this. She may caution her family not to sit "here" or "there" for fear of their disturbing the house. She may serve TV dinners and insist that the family eat out frequently; she is simply too busy with her housework to cook. Still, a third housewife may say "nuts" to the menial tasks, insist that togetherness is what counts, and spend much time with her family doing enjoyable things. If all were forced to spend an equal amount of time and effort at each of the roles attached to the status of housewife, they would all three most likely find the job to be intolerable. It would, under that set of stringent regulations, not permit any individuality.

The status of the teacher holds relatively constant in the larger society; however, the person filling that position tends to perform relatively different roles, depending upon where he or she is at a given moment.[37] Thus, there are certain roles attached to the teacher's behavior within the classroom. There is another set of roles attached to the teacher's behavior in the school, and finally still another set of roles attached to the teacher's behavior in the community-at-large. In short, it may be assumed that teachers have three rather clearly distinct role-sets attached to their status as teachers: (1) classroom role-set, (2) school role-set, and (3) community-at-large role-set. They appear to differentiate among these sets of roles and to specialize to a great degree. It appears that they concentrate largely on the first two in carrying out the role behavior of teachers. It appears that teachers also tend to emphasize certain roles within each of these role-sets. Few are probably able to give equal attention and effort to all the roles included in any one role-set. Doubtlessly, the teachers' tendency to specialize or emphasize one or two roles in the classroom or in the school is influenced by such factors as type of teacher training experienced, social class origins, occupational experience, subject area competency, and situational variables. Teachers appear to differ significantly in the classroom situation as to the type of learning experience they feel desirable for students. One teacher may act in a manner which emphasizes her role as inculcator of formalized knowledge; another may regard the socialization of students as the chief task. A third may view the development of creativity and innovative thinking on the part of the students as the major task. Other teachers may feel different roles are more important in the job of classroom teaching; still others may combine two or more types of classroom roles and act as generalists.

Thus, the A type teachers give priority in their classroom behavior to the conveyance of formalized knowledge. The A type teacher often treats the students in a "no-nonsense manner." He or she frequently insists that the students are there to learn. Such teachers feel pride when students evidence acquisition of formal knowledge. The teacher with this role orientation may point with pride to the number of National Merit Scholarship winners who have passed through her class. She often insists that the class begin on time; time wasted is time not spent learning. She does not look with favor upon those who habitually forget their assignments or who turn them in late. Frequently, teachers who emphasize their classroom role as purveyors of formal knowledge are regarded, and not without pride, by many of the students as the "toughest" teachers in the building. Selection of students for membership in the National Honor Society is important to her. On the day of Honors Convocation she may beam as her students troop across the stage to receive their awards in the *Reader's Digest* annual poetry contest. Such teachers may be very good or very bad, or any degree in between in quality of teaching; their emphasis on using the classroom to convey formalized knowledge simply reflects their orientation toward various roles open to the classroom teacher.

The B type teacher emphasizes the role of teacher as socializing agent. Frequently, formalized knowledge is viewed by this type teacher as not especially relevant; and priority is given to helping the students in their life-adjustment processes. While he may teach English, math, history or physical education, his overriding orientation is toward explorations in solutions to life problems. He may often slide upon the desk, dismiss the regular class assignment, and discuss or lecture at length on the aspects of life he confronted in World War II, the Korean conflict, or the Vietnam War. Or, indeed, he may discuss the difficulties faced by Frederick the Great in his wars with Russia, Austria, and the German principalities. He does not mean to convey names, dates, or historical events, but rather to use the material to socialize the students. The subject area he is teaching may have a close relationship to this overall emphasis or it may not. He often tosses the book "out the window." He feels that the students need to develop healthy social attitudes — to become self-directed. He acts in a manner that emphasizes the student adviser role of the teacher's classroom role-set. He may read little; his greatest efforts are directed toward student advisement in social problems, and he may be available at any time, day or night, for this task. He may quite intentionally drop by the service station in order to talk with one of the gas pump jockeys about the merits of his returning to school to obtain a high school diploma. Frequently, B type teachers enjoy many of the extracurricular activities such as ticket-taking, etc., abhorred by other instructors. He views it as an opportunity to advise and counsel with present and former students. Possibily, the B type teachers tend to slow down the learning process, and in this action, they permit the "late bloomer" and the slow learner to adjust to the educational process. Again, the actual quality of teaching of B types may be of any level, from brilliant to inane.

The C type teacher views her job as an opportunity to produce creativity and innovative behavior in the students. She definitely "hears a different drummer." The C type teacher is usually highly individualistic and is often a nonconformist. He or she may be highly artistic. As an English teacher, the C type may deemphasize the importance of correct spelling, punctuation, etc., and emphasize the desirability of expressing an original thought, idea, or image in a paper. Such teachers may, in studying poetry, emphasize the visual aspects of that form of writing and take the class to watch the grain rolling in the fields in the manner of the sea before the wind. He or she may, in addition, take the students to the gymnasium in order to watch the basketball players in warm-up exercises prior to their scrimmaging. She may use this as evidence of the relationship between physical patterns and poetry. A C type coach might insist that prior to reporting for football practice, each player complete a course in ballet. He might feel such a course produces good timing, rhythm, and coordination. An art teacher with a C type orientation in a Midwestern city decided to take her students in advanced art to the local morgue, in order to provide them the opportunity to better study anatomy and thus to gain an idea as to the actual color of flesh and the elements which composed that color. While they were there, they were given permission by the attendant to carve a bit on the bodies. The teacher and students did so. Upon arrival at school the next day, the teacher was requested by the principal to attend a private conference with him and the superintendent. The teacher attempted to explain that working on cadavers had been part of the art training of Leonardo da Vinci, Michelangelo, and Raphael and that they had not done too badly. The principal was not impressed, and the superintendent insisted that students could learn to draw anatomy from stick figures provided by the supply office.

There are possibly many other role orientations emphasized by teachers in their classroom role-set. Since one of the basic functions of the instructor is to evaluate students, it appears possible that some teachers give priority to this role in their classroom work. Speculation suggests that such type D teachers spend long hours on devising and validating testing materials. They keep charts and scores on their students, not only for the present year but for many preceding years. They are pleased when a student in one of their classes is able to achieve the highest score made in the chemistry class in the ten years that the test has been given. They may spend a great amount of time doing item analyses of the test questions they have used. Grade points and mean scores are considered very important, and every student in the D type teacher's classroom is made acutely aware of the difference between an 85 and an 86 score. The D type, as projected here, simply is oriented toward the evaluation tasks in the role-set of teachers and has tended to specialize in it. In a world in which industrial-technological specialization is encouraged, it is logical to assume relatively similar behavior on the part of educators.

Since there are many other basic roles in the teacher's classroom role-set, one may analyze the degree to which other teachers specialize. Thus, we may have the disciplinarian; the super-spy, who knows just what has happened and where the most likely suspect is to be found. There may be orientations toward such roles as that of custodian. Here the individual emphasizes the necessity of a clean and healthful room. The chalkboards must be freshly washed, the windows open, the lights on. Indeed, such types are likely to win the "Best Bulletin Board of the Year Award." Doubtlessly, there are groups of teachers who emphasize two or more of the roles in their classroom role-set. We may refer to these as hybrid role types or generalists, as distinguished from those who emphasize the importance of one role. The latter may be labeled purists.

While it is merely speculative, it is assumed by the writers that among the purist types, the A type teacher is apt to predominate. The A and B type roles are relatively "safe." The general public and school administrators probably think of these behavioral roles as the proper domain of all teachers. They accept these role concepts or orientations on the part of teachers as being legitimate. The C, D, or other type orientations may find a somewhat colder reception on the part of administrators and the public. It is interesting to consider the possibility that teachers tend to gravitate in their career patterns to schools where great toleration is permitted for their particular teaching behavior, role orientations.

Much research is needed in validating the concept of role and role-set. However, it is apparent that where there is great variance between the roles emphasized by teachers and the role expectations held by the students for teachers, we will find role conflict, low job satisfaction, and low student morale. Possibilities of physical violence are not ruled out. Causes for much of the disturbances observed on college and university campuses between 1968 and 1971 may be based upon differences in role expectations held by professors and students and between students and administrators. From an observer's point of view it appeared during this period of time that students frequently listed as part of their demanded reforms the hiring of more professors to function as B type classroom teachers. On the secondary school level, role conflict can probably be found in situations in which the teacher emphasizes the role of teacher as socializing agent and where the students, possibly from wealthy middle-class suburban areas, expect the teacher to act as inculcator of formalized knowledge. In this situation the students expect the teacher to help them acquire sufficient formal knowledge to gain admission to a prestigious college or university. It is hypothesized that physical violence will be evidenced in situations in which A type teachers attempt to enforce their role orientations upon students who primarily need the influence and help of B type instructors. One can but speculate on the outcome when the principal or other school administrators feel that all teachers should be of A or B type and discover that a C type is on the faculty; they will probably not be long in discovering this fact. On the other hand, it may be hypothesized type C teachers are attracted to experimental type schools where consideration is given for nonconformity and where indeed, such teacher behavior is often highly rewarded.

The great likelihood of role specialization on the part of teachers in their classroom role-set raises grave questions regarding such professional matters as merit pay. Which type is the really good teacher? The purist, the hybrid, or the complete generalist? If it is the purist, which type, A, B, C, D, etc., should be rated highest? Or must the best teachers be complete generalists who combine a wide variety of roles from the classroom role-set? Merit pay, under conditions of role specialization, appears to make little sense. Teacher ratings by students may also be a questionable practice if great amounts of role specialization exist. Those students with expectations that the teacher will "get down to business" and teach formalized knowledge may rate a B type teacher extremely poorly; conversely their ratings of an A type who fulfills their expectations may be very high. Students who are "late bloomers" or slow learners may be greatly benefited by a B type teacher and may rate him or her quite highly and condemn both A and C types. It would appear that students are very likely to give extremely poor ratings to teachers when there is a lack of consensus between teachers and students on the role behavior of the teacher.

The teacher has a set of roles attached to his work as a teacher in the school as well as a set attached to his work in the classroom. These school roles may be affected to a large extent by his age, length of teaching experience, sex, subject area of specialization, amount of formalized education, etc. Thus, a male teacher who has taught for 15 years in college preparatory English in the high school and has earned his doctorate may play significantly different roles within the high school than does a first-year teacher in home economics who has a temporary teaching license and has yet to complete a bachelor's degree. The roles of individuals such as home economics teacher, athletic coach, and industrial arts teacher may differ significantly from those in the core academic areas. In addition, these teachers often do not operate out of the central building but work in different buildings or off-rooms. Their relatively greater isolation may operate to eliminate some of the roles contained in the school role-set of other teachers.

The teacher's school role-set is usually considered to include work in the areas of academic advising, sponsoring extracurricular activities, counseling, clerical work, committee duties, departmental assignments, working as a colleague with other faculty members, being a subject-area specialist, and doing in-service training as well as working as a classroom teacher. The role-set of the college or university teacher on this level of behavior usually includes work as researcher, teaching, administering, committee duties, guest lecturing, serving as subject area specialist, clerical duties, etc. Yamamoto and Dizney suggest that four types of college-wide roles are involved in the professor's job. They specify these as teaching, research work, socializing, and administration work.[38] Knapp indicates in his research that the college professor in America has been asked to perform three quite different roles or functions which he designated as (1) research function, (2) the informational function, and (3) the character-building function.[39] He indicates that these functions or roles are becoming increasingly incompatible and lead to role conflict for the professor.[40] Monson has analyzed the college teacher's roles as those of scholar, consultant, teacher, and administrator.[41] Gustad similarly suggests that the professor has several roles, which he lists as (1) individual, (2) teacher, (3) scholar and researcher, (4) organization man, (5) member of academic community, and (6) member of the community-at-large.[42] Finally, in an excellent theoretical framework, Biddle and Thomas suggest that on the basis of their role behavior professors may be divided into two basic divisions: (1) generalists and (2) specialists. While specialists' roles may be formed by emphasizing the role of (1) teacher, (2) researcher, (3) administrator, or (4) service, a generalist will combine several of these roles in his behavior in carrying out his office.[43]

In an effort to test the above assumption that college teachers do specialize in their role behavior, the writers along with Dr. Sing-Nan Fen in 1969 investigated the degree to which 192 college teachers of education emphasized various roles in their professional work. The study hypothesized that college teachers of education would tend to emphasize one of the following roles in their academic behavior, or they might combine two or more of the roles and be a generalist. The roles were: (1) teacher, (2) researcher, (3) administrator, and (4) professional. This last role type indicated concern with, and involvement in, the affairs of the profession or academic area of specialization such as history of education, philosophy of education, etc. Evidence of this last role was measured as amount of time the man or woman devoted to "pushing" the subject area and expanding its influence and recognition. The data in Table I indicate that it is difficult for college teachers of education to function in several diverse roles within their academic work. The pure specialists who focused their behavior on one role comprise 64.08 percent of the total sample, while the two-role hybrid types compose 23.43 percent, and the three-role hybrid types make up only 12.5 percent of the total group. No individual in the sample was able to distribute his efforts equally across all the designated roles.

The process of carrying out the roles attached to the status position is referred to by sociologists of education as role enactment. In this role enactment, it appears that teachers, and possibly educators in general,

TABLE I

Role Specialization of College Teachers of Education at
Eight Midwestern Institutions

Role Type	Number	Percentage
T (Teacher)	97	50.52
R (Researcher)	15	7.82
A (Administrator)	8	4.17
P (Professional)	3	1.57
Totals for one-item types	123	64.08
TR (Teacher-Researcher)	13	6.77
TA (Teacher-Administrator)	11	5.73
TP (Teacher-Professional)	8	4.17
RT (Researcher-Teacher)	9	4.69
AP (Administrator-Professional)	3	1.57
PT (Professional-Teacher)	1	.50
Totals for two-item types	45	23.43
TRA	1	.52
TRP	2	1.05
TAR	1	.52
TAP	1	.52
TPR	2	1.05
TPA	2	1.05
RTP	2	1.05
RPT	1	.52
RPA	2	1.05
ATR	2	1.05
ATP	1	.52
ART	1	.52
APT	1	.52
PTA	4	2.09
PRT	1	.52
Totals for three-item types	24	12.50

operate from certain very general orientations or points of view that are
reflected in their behavior on every level including classroom roles,
school roles, and community-at-large roles. It appears that some teachers
have a localistic orientation in enacting the roles, whereas other teachers
operate largely from a cosmopolitan view.[44] The teacher who enacts his
or her role-sets in such a manner as to reflect a localistic orientation
tends to emphasize in his behavior the importance of the local community. He becomes a regular participant in the community's affairs.
Often in his class work he uses examples taken from the local scene. His
anecdotal stories and illustrations emphasize the local area and region.
This becomes his starting point in class lectures and discussions. Last
night's basketball game or football contest becomes the elements of class
discussion prior to beginning work on the day's assignment. He may

spend a great amount of time talking local problems in the teachers' lounge or playing cards with the coaches in their offices. He is aware of the backgrounds of many members of the student body and is familiar with many of their relatives. He has usually spent much of his life in the area in which he teaches. To the contrary, it appears that those who orient toward a cosmopolitan manner of role enactment tend to emphasize the national and international scene in their classes and in the school. Their role-sets reflect their interest and concern with the larger world. They may require the students to read from the *Wall Street Journal* and insist that the school subscribe to *The New York Times*. Their assignments to students accent their concern with world culture. Often, the cosmopolitan teacher is not regarded as a part of the regular community. Such teachers appear aloof from the commonplace. Hence the role behavior that either the localist or cosmopolitan displays in the classroom, school, or community reflects his basic perceptions of the professional status of teachers. Such diversity of views is probably influenced by family backgrounds, social class origins, types of educational institutions attended, and especially by areas of academic specialization.

Another orientation of teachers reflected in their role behavior is the degree to which educators view their status as being that of (1) professional or (2) public servant.[45] Teachers who interpret the status as being akin to that of public servant will reflect this in their role behavior. In such instances, the teacher may first ascertain the public's reaction to the use of controversial novels in her English class prior to requiring them to be read by her students. The public servant type teacher checks "to the power" and rarely acts in a manner to defy the constituted authority or public opinion. Such teachers will not question the right of the administration to assign them extracurricular tasks such as taking tickets at athletic events or carrying on charity drives in or out of school. Chain of command is important to this type teacher. When rules and regulations are formulated at the level of the superintendency or school board, the public servant type teacher does not question them, but carries them out often in a ritualistic manner. This type of teacher simply views himself as a public employee and feels that in a democratic society it is essential for such employees to carry out the desires of the people. He may personally disagree with some policies; however, he feels that he must represent majority opinion in his professional conduct.

Some teachers appear to perceive the role and role-set of educators from a professional orientation. They see teachers as professionals and, therefore, ethically and legally feel that they may operate without great interference from other sources. Thus, they feel that they, as professionals, have a right to decide what is best for their own classrooms and for their areas of academic specialization. They tend not to consult with others but to inform them of their actions or intentions. The professional type frequently insists that teachers are ultimately responsible and therefore must make the greater part of the decisions. They view such groups as the PTA as functioning to carry out and implement the ideas of the educators. On the other hand, the localist type teacher views the PTA as voicing public opinion. Therefore, programs and projects can originate with such groups, and educators must help carry them out. The professionals tend to regard themselves in much the same manner as they regard physicians or lawyers. They are viewed as experts in their respective areas of endeavor, and while the public has a right to ask for their opinions and help, the professionals as experts have views that must carry heavier weight than those who do not have such expertise.

Informal Role Behavior of Educators

There are formal and informal roles enacted by teachers and other educators. It is possible that in large bureaucratic organizational structures it is necessary that informal roles exist for individuals. Such roles provide the flexibility necessary for such structures to function adequately. The strictly formal roles such as teacher, counselor, school administrator, etc., appear to be locked in to certain relatively rigid sets of expectations. It is sometimes suggested that the formal role behavior is enmeshed in routines, regulations, and rules. There is too much "red-tape" for adequate functioning in many situations.[46] In order to make the whole organizational structure more effective and permit individuals to function properly, it appears necessary that many informal roles develop among the personnel employed in the organization. These informal roles are acted out in the teachers' lounge, the boiler room, the coach's office, the place where the principal eats lunch, or in any informal setting that can be devised by the educators. The enactment of these informal roles tends to relieve pressures generated by the formal structure. In short, through enactment of informal roles, one frequently has an opportunity to get rid of aggression or act in a manner that would probably not be permitted in the formal roles or role-sets. Second, these informal roles, since they are not officially recognized or sanctioned,

serve as a means for conveying messages, ideas, grievances, and acknowl-
edgments that could otherwise not be expressed. Frequently, the informal roles enacted among educators serve as the "lubricating oil" in
the organizational machinery. One uses these informal roles to cut "red
tape" and get the job done. The informal roles act as a sort of weather
vane to any administrator or educator. Close observation of the informal
roles can inform the personnel of approaching dangers and warn them
of the level of "blood pressure" of the organization as a whole.

Anyone who has taught for any length of time on the elementary,
secondary, or higher educational levels is well aware of the various informal roles that are developed among staff and faculty members. A mere
listing of these indicates their utilitarian nature:

1. The Detective (Knows exactly who is having domestic problems, informs
personnel of this; relates past educators' problems; always ready to reveal the
inside secrets of students or faculty).

2. The Matchmaker (Wants to get people together; knows just the person
you should meet. Gets bang out of school romances.)

3. Ego-Supporter (Tells you what a grand job you are doing; relates comments from others or outsiders about your fine abilities, etc.)

4. Mediator (Is expected to step into argument and compromise it; tries to
patch things up. Often expects to be asked for advice on personnel problems.)

5. Medical Practitioner (Notes you are not looking well; advises that you
take particular vitamins or see her physician; possibly you need a remedy she
can supply.)

6. The Bitcher (Complains constantly about everything and everyone.
Leaves you wondering why she ever went into teaching in first place, and second, why she stayed.)

7. The Friend (Helps you settle down and gain perspective; tells you it is
no unique problem but happens to almost all teachers; discreet and doesn't
repeat; relaxes you.)

8. The Romeo (Flirts needlessly; makes a play for everyone of opposite
sex; is perennially "on the make." Thinks everyone is attracted to him or her.)

9. The Tattletale (Runs like mad to relate anything to the administration;
can't be trusted.)

10. The Moral Crusader (Always has a cause going; evangelicalism runs
rampant; wants you to join in her cause; wakes up every morning with a new
crusade.)

It is probable that on each level of role enactment — classroom,
school, and community-at-large—there are informal roles developed that
aid the educator in carrying out his more formalized roles. The informal

roles act in such a manner as to permit much individuality to be displayed that could otherwise not exist within the formal role behavior. These informal roles also provide others surrounding the incumbent of the position a means of more accurately predicting his behavior and what may be expected of him in the formal roles. In addition, the informal roles provide a means by which tensions, anxieties, and neuroses may be released without penalty. Because they are released through informal role behavior, they are not official, and cannot, therefore, be recognized as legitimate. Rarely can negative or positive sanctions be administered toward such informal role behavior. This behavior is "above the law" because the actions cannot, strictly speaking, be proved.

There are behaviors in any bureaucratic structure that are detrimental to the operations of the organization. Informal roles played by certain educational personnel may be detrimental to the operations of the school. Sociologists of education refer to these behaviors as dysfunctional roles.[47] Of course, what is dysfunctional to one element of the school's population may be viewed as very functional to another element. While the teachers may act in an informal manner to slow down the work that the administrators have requested on reports or committee work, this may be considered dysfunctional by the administration but quite functional by the teachers, who feel the administrator is a "slave driver" trying to get himself promoted at their expense by claiming credit for the work they are doing. The teachers may simply ignore an assistant principal. They "play dumb" when he asks them about any situation and they ignore his requests to do something. To the assistant principal such behavior is dysfunctional; however, to the teachers who are practicing it, it is very functional, since it is intended to either get rid of the guy who must secure their cooperation or to reform him and to "check" his power.[48]

The School Administrator's Status and Role

Many concepts involving the status and role of schoolteachers and college teachers are applicable to the principal and superintendent. However, the relatively greater amount of visibility of the school administrators in the community-at-large and the unique status of these individuals in the middle levels of management in large bureaucratic organizations present problems of status and role not usually experienced by purely teaching personnel. Table II indicates the

TABLE II

COMPARSION OF ROLE AREAS OF SPECIALIZATION FOR TEACHERS,
PRINCIPALS, AND SUPERINTENDENTS

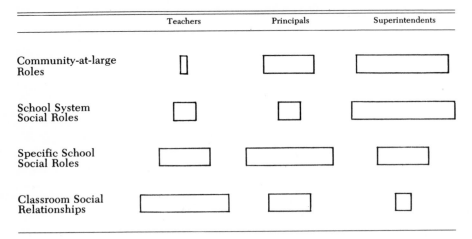

comparative role relationships existent for teachers, principals, and superintendents. This differential division of labor in the school system dictates relatively different role expectations, role behavior, and role-sets.

To understand the roles of the principal and superintendent, it is essential to understand the bureaucratic nature of the positions (statuses) that these administrators hold. Max Weber was the first to attempt to develop a theory of bureaucratic organizations.[49] While much of his work centered on government and business structures, the concepts which he projected appear to be applicable to the school as a bureaucratic organization. He noted that the functions of a bureaucracy are distributed in extremely fixed ways and labeled as official duties.[50] In short, such structures tend to codify very explicitly the role behavior of the men and women who hold the status positions. Such codification is intended to insure a minimum amount of overlapping in duties attached to particular statuses and thus prevent personal antagonism as much as possible. Such structuring, it is assumed, tends to create conditions for high efficiency and productivity. The principal and superintendent are, according to such theory, locked into the structure and their role behavior is highly codified. The teacher appears not to be subject to these regulations to the same extent.

Miller and Woock have indicated that, in bureaucratic structures such as schools, the duties are clearly stated and defined and well known to all who hold status within these organizations.[51] Weber has noted that in a bureaucracy there is a hierarchy of positions (statuses), with the next higher level having responsibility for the next lower level with regard to assigning tasks, hiring and firing, and promotions.[52] Thus, the individual in the status position immediately higher than one's own can, if he chooses, dictate to a large extent the functions and role behavior which one below him will carry out. Sociologists of education refer to those holding higher status in the bureaucratic structure than one's own as superordinates. Those holding such status below one's own position are termed subordinates. Thus, the school board instructs the superintendent, who in turn instructs the principals. Principals in turn instruct the teachers and teachers instruct the students. One difficulty that may arise in any bureaucracy is that as a result of a great amount of specialization (each status is assigned specific tasks and no others) there frequently tends to be a lack of communication.[53] One division does not know what the other is doing. Therefore, role expectations outside the code are difficult to ascertain, or as the situation changes, there may be no code to indicate appropriate role behavior.

While the rules and regulations that make the bureaucracy functional are often laid down in a concrete form, they are thought sufficient to solve most problems. The incumbents of the positions are expected to carry them out.[54] These rules and regulations not only include directives on how outside problems should be treated but also define the responsibility of each person in the bureaucratic structure and his appropriate relationship with other people.[55] To a great degree, the bureaucratic organization is locked into a relatively formalistic framework which can be changed only slowly and whose personnel—in this instance, principals and superintendents—are expected to be effective in carrying out school policy and programs. One of the merits of the "organization man" is reputed to be his ability to get things done and to be highly productive. In this effort, the organizational role behavior as codified in most institutions holds that personal and subjective behavior be kept to an absolute minimum. Such administrative personnel must attempt, at all costs, to deal with all people and all situations in a completely objective manner. Thus, we basically tend to think of the "establishment" as being

cold, hard, and lacking in emotional concern. One of the writers recalls
that as part of the National Principalship Study conducted by Dr. Neal
Gross, then of Harvard University, hundreds of principals across the
United States were interviewed and asked their opinions concerning
their role behavior and their perceptions of the role expectations held
for them by their superordinates and subordinates. One principal interviewed in a large city system noted that he had never personally met
with the superintendent and that he had seen him only once other than
on television or in the newspaper. This occasion had been a formal dinner that had taken place in a large hotel some seven years prior to the
interview. One can sense the difficulty in attempting to identify the role
behavior desired by his superordinate when one has little access to him.
Even the informal role behavior among top administrators which is used
to dispel anxieties and tensions in the bureaucratic structures would be
extremely difficult to achieve.

A lack of understanding or communications noted by Weber appears
to exist for many principals. Again, one of the writers in the National
Principalship Study recalls interviewing a principal who indicated that
he was never consulted by the superintendent, owing to the large size
of the school system, and that he had found that the only means to career
advancement was the production of National Merit Scholarship winners
in his school. It appeared that this type of productivity tended to relate
to pay increases and promotions to larger schools. However, he wasn't
too sure. In an effort to turn out such products, he had all of his senior
students screened early in the year and selected some two dozen who
he felt were capable of winning such honors. Incidentally, he was in a
school located in an urban ghetto, and he noted the unfairness of the
assumed promotional criteria, since some principals were assigned to
wealthy, suburban areas where the students often were able to win the
scholarships with a minimum amount of effort on the part of the faculty
and staff. He indicated that after screening the students, he installed
coke, pop, and candy machines in the school and collected the profits
from this enterprise. In addition, he charged the students five cents to
attend noontime intramural athletic events. The school had unusually
good intramural teams and much interest centered on these contests.
From these combined proceeds, he hired some of his better teachers to
remain after school or to return on Saturday to tutor the preselected
senior students. All of this appeared to be totally unknown to the principal's superordinates. He noted with some pride that he had produced

five National Merit Scholarship winners in his school, whereas none had ever been produced in the prior history of the school. This incident suggests that where formal codes of role behavior are extremely stringent or where they are impossible to fulfill because they are unknown, or the size of the institution forbids it, etc., informal means will be devised and instituted in order to "cut red tape" or circumvent the impossible rules designed by a distant or unreasonable superior.

Because principals and superintendents and other administrative personnel operate in relatively large organizational structures, various types of role conflict may develop for them. Miller and Woock suggest that conflict may develop when one unit achieves autonomy and becomes relatively independent from the other units within the organization.[56] Conflict may develop between personnel of different ranks within the linear structure of the organization; thus, the principal comes into conflict with an assistant superintendent.[57] Horizontal role conflict would be evidenced when units or personnel of the same rank disagree. Securing role consensus among many staff and faculty members in a bureaucratic organization is no simple matter. The bureaucratic structure is so designed as to eliminate as much as possible such conflict by depersonalizing much of the decision making and program planning.

Undoubtedly much variation in role behavior of principals and superintendents occurs as a result of differences in size of systems in which they operate. Most textbooks on school administration divide the systems into three types: small, medium, and large. Neal Gross and Robert Herriott attempted in their study of staff leadership in public schools to investigate the effects of Executive Professional Leadership (EPL) of elementary public school principals upon the functioning of the school. They found a positive relationship between EPL of principals' and teachers' morale, their professional performance, and the pupils' learning.[58] An interesting finding of the study was that concerning the relationship between size of student body and EPL. "It was shown that the smaller the school enrollment, the greater the principal's EPL."[59] In short, it appears that smaller school enrollments gave the principal greater opportunity to assert good leadership. In their conclusions Gross and Herriott suggested that certain credentials on the part of elementary principals were related to high EPL:

To sum up these implications of our study: if Executive Professional Leadership is to be the criterion, many school systems are selecting principals on grounds that appear to have little empirical justification: type or amount of teaching experience, experience as an assistant or vice principal, number of undergraduate and graduate courses in education, number of graduate courses in educational administration, sex, and marital status. On the other hand, characteristics that should be preferred in appointing elementary principals are: a high level of academic performance in college, a high order of inter-personal skill, the motive of service, the willingness to commit off-duty time to their work, and relatively little seniority as teachers.[60]

This last quality is especially interesting. Apparently, to have played the role of classroom teacher for a long period of time resulted in the incumbent's inability to shift role behavior when he or she moved into the status of principal. Possibly, such individuals with long tenure in one position tend to internalize the roles appropriate for that status and are unable to adopt new behavior. This is probably especially true for those teachers who specialize in one or two roles of the teacher's role-sets. Those with more balance or hybridization may be able to make better adjustments.

While wide variation exists with respect to the principal's formal role behavior owing to differences in size of schools and level of schools, generally speaking the role-set attached to the principal's position in his building are supervisor of custodial services, supervisor of instruction in the building, director of personnel, pupil control, in-service training for teachers, controller of health programs, and motivator. The aspects of behavior attached to his role-set in the community-at-large appear to be public relations, working with community agencies, communicating objectives of the school to the public, obtaining parental cooperation with the school, etc. It appears that the typical principal has little part in the actual classroom teaching. He operates here in a rather indirect manner except in cases of pupil control or teacher incompetence.

The role-sets of the superintendency appear to divide along the lines of instruction and business. The collection of sub-roles he must perform either directly or indirectly include finance manager, personnel director, supervisor of instruction, business manager, public relations expert, record keeper and clerk, purchasing agent, morale booster, athletic director, etc. Francis Merrill indicates that managerial personnel tend to function in three ways and thus possess three different role-sets. The superintendent appears to fit into the role-sets described by Merrill; he functions as (1) technician, (2) manager, and (3) supervisor. As technician the superintendent tends to "process" human beings. In this effort he instructs, supervises, appraises, and promotes people.[61] In the managerial role he "mediates" between elements in the organization and between elements within and without the school organization.[62] Finally, the superintendent acts in a supervisory role, and in this effort he is concerned with overseeing the aims and objectives of the entire school system. He is responsible for policy making in the broadest sense.[63]

The orientations of school administrators to the positions which they hold are reflected to a great extent in their role behavior and their conduct in many of their role-sets. One might suggest that it is at this point that philosophy tends to link up with sociology of education. The orientations may be related to early experiences, years spent in other academic positions, social class origins, values held, etc. In any case, school administrators appear to have basically different philosophic attitudes or orientations toward their position and the nature of the school system. We may, therefore, have some administrators who view themselves as earth-smoothers, whereas others view their position as earth-shakers. The earth-smoother tends to restrict those who would charge off in the direction of reform. He is a modifier. He is a conciliator and an arbitrator. He plays in his public school relationships the same role as exemplified by Dwight David Eisenhower as President of the United States. Standing in contradistinction to earth-smoothers are those administrators who view themselves as earth-shakers and who attempt constant change. They are the "doers." They create tension, excitement, and anxiety. They are basically the reformers in any structure. These reforms may be of the "across the board" type, or they may consist in one major reform each year.

Another role orientation dividing many school administrators is the degree to which one follows the codified behavior of the bureaucracy. Thus, one administrator may be a loose constructionist, whereas another is a strict constructionist. The former does as he pleases so long as the code does not specifically state that he cannot take such action. On the other hand, the strict constructionist tends to follow the rules in a ritualistic manner and will not do anything unless the code states specifically that he can do so. Obviously, the principal referred to earlier in this chapter who instituted a method for producing National Merit Scholarship winners in his school was a loose constructionist. This dimension relates closely to the one applied to teaching personnel that divided them along professional and public servant orientations.

Other role orientations on which administrators appear to differ in their behavior is the degree to which the incumbent is democratic or

autocratic in his decision-making policies. In short, he may be consulta-
tive or directive in his policies. He may similarly be a supporter of cen-
tralization or a supporter of decentralization. That is, he may gather the
power into his own hands or he may farm it out to different school elements. By placing principals and superintendents somewhere along a
continuum of each of these orientations, we can achieve a profile of his
role orientation as administrator.[64]

Student Status and Roles

Research work in analyzing student status and roles has been relatively restricted despite the importance of these factors for all educators
and school systems. Notable research has been done in this area by A. B.
Hollingshead, who studied Elmtown High School in the early 1940s,[65]
by C. Wayne Gordon, who published *The Social System of the High
School* in 1957,[66] by James S. Coleman, who published *The Adolescent
Society* in 1961,[67] by Burton R. Clark, who wrote an interesting chapter
on the sub-cultures of youth in his *Educating the Expert Society* in
1962,[68] and by Talcott Parsons in "Youth in the Context of American
Society."[69] It is surprising to discover that most analyses of student status
and roles contain examinations or reexamination of material originally
published in the above works. It is possible that much later work was
not done simply because of the tumultuous conditions surrounding students in the late 1960s and early 1970s. The student disturbances on
high school and college campuses and the volatility of situations possibly
made it extremely difficult to gain reliable measures of student attitudes
and student behavior. That which was published during this time was of
a sermonizing nature.

Hollingshead early discovered that much of the student behavior as
reflected in status and roles was based upon the socioeconomic status
(SES) of the parents.[70] His work done in the early 1940s apparently did
accurately register the significance of the family's social position upon
the student's status and roles at that time. Thus, having the "right" kind
of home to which fellow students could be invited, having nice clothing,
spending money, and having influential parents acted as determinants
of the position and roles one would play inside the school. He viewed
parental social class membership in the larger community as the major
determinant of the student's school success.[71] Thus, most children from
the lower-middle and upper-middle classes tended to be enrolled in the

college preparatory curricula. If one's parents were low on the SES scale, then he or she had little opportunity to play important roles in the school or enjoy high status positions. The curricula at this time appeared to be divided among those in the college preparatory, the general education, and the technical and industrial arts type classes.[72] Students were grouped in various brackets according to the parental status in the community.[73] Hollingshead attributed this close relationship between social class membership and academic success to the educators' awareness of the power positions which the parents of the students occupied in the community.[74] Studies of this same period indicate that the grades given for academic achievement tended to relate directly to the social class membership of students.[75] In short, it appeared to be a period when teachers and other educators in the aftermath of the economic depression, 1929-39, gave primacy in dealing with students to the social structure, and hence the power structure, of the community. Many communities were small enough for knowledge of community leaders to be acquired by the teachers and educators. More recently, some writers and researchers have looked back in a nostalgic way and suggested that in the period of the 1940s teachers and educators were decisive influences in designating students' statuses and role behavior. Probably, this was not true; the teachers merely reflected the prevailing status quo of the community and acted in such a manner as to implement it.

Apparently, a somewhat different phenomenon developed in the mid-1950s and early 1960s. The youth culture came into being. Burton Clark refers to it as the "youth culture;"[76] James Coleman labels it "adolescent sub-culture."[77] Irrespective of designation, this youth culture began to emerge as a powerful socializing agent in its own right during this period. Coleman suggests that the development of the student culture was inevitable. "To summarize: in a rapidly changing, highly rationalized society, the 'natural processes' of education in the family are no longer adequate."[78] Sarane Boocock notes that the family has tended to fragment and lose many of its older and more basic functions, and now the educational institution not only has extended itself into teaching a greater amount of technical and industrial type learning but has added enormously to the degree to which it attempts to inculcate values, morality, and dispositions in the students.[79] Evidence of this latter function is revealed in an examination of the school's programs in drug abuse, sex education, courses on marriage and the family, homemaking, consumer economics, etc. Discussions in a senior problems class often are oriented toward morality and legality in the society and in the personal lives of the students. Boocock notes that the school as a bureaucratic organization is unable to provide the individualistic support the family was formally able to give.[80] A bureaucracy has too many rules and regulations and is too depersonalized to function in this manner. Cut off from former means of socialization, the student is, according to Coleman, " 'cut off' from the rest of society, forced inward toward his own age group, made to carry out his whole life with others his own age. With his fellows, he comes to constitute a small society, one that has most of its important interactions *within* itself, and maintains only a few threads of connections with the outside adult society."[81] Thus, from Hollingshead to Coleman, a period of 20 years, a dramatic change apparently occurred with respect to control of student status and roles.

Clark suggests that three sub-cultures have emerged as a result of this new phenomenon of youth culture. These he labels as the fun sub-culture, the academic sub-culture, and the delinquent sub-culture.[82] Within the school there appears to be a wide range of roles which the students may play. Some of these roles are attached to the classroom situation; others are related to the total school and are more macroscopic in nature; and last, it appears that some roles extend over into the community-at-large. Students within the youth culture appear to emphasize or specialize in roles that focus on one of the three situations. In general, to be a class brain, a grind, to have the smarts, to be a curve raiser, a booker, etc., is to focus one's role behavior primarily on the roles or role-set attached to the classroom situation. On the other hand, the large majority of students in most recent studies have tended to emphasize or specialize in the role-set or roles attached to student behavior in the larger school setting. In this instance, emphasis is placed on all-school activities and events such as social groups, athletics, the right crowd, being popular, being elected Prom Queen, Yearbook Queen, Football Queen, doing Flirtation Walk with a popular member of the opposite sex, parking a nice car in the school lot, etc. Students who prefer to emphasize or specialize in this domain of role behavior appear to relate closely to what Clark labels the fun sub-culture.[83] Last, the writers feel that what Clark labels as the "delinquent sub-culture" in reality can be designated as including those students who emphasize in their behavior the roles exemplified in the larger community, such as the street-corner society, the hoods, the drug addicts, the criminal element in society, etc.[84] But in addition to these, this group more recently includes many who voice the views of the Peace Movement, Anti-War groups, Jesus Freaks, etc. They take their roles from social groups outside the school and emphasize them within the classroom and school. They are often blatant in presenting these views and reflect them in their selection of roles available in the youth culture.

Of course, the selection of one or more of these role-sets is not merely a matter of chance nor of will. The ability to specialize in some of these roles may depend upon natural endowment such as athletic ability, academic ability, physical attractiveness, talents, skills, etc. The individual is not completely free to select what he would desire to emphasize; however, it appears from Coleman's study that teachers and other educators have little power in designating the statuses or roles or endowing any special ones with esteem or prestige.[85] The youth culture appears capable of doing this without outside influence. Indeed, as most studies indicate, the teachers and educators appear singularly "out of it" with respect to knowledge of and skills in dealing with the youth culture.

Coleman did his research in Illinois in the heartland of high school basketball country.[86] He found that for boys, the elite in descending order tended to be composed of (1) boys who were both top athletes and top scholars, (2) boys who were top athletes, (3) boys who were top scholars, and (4) boys who were neither top athletes nor top scholars. He found that boys who were either athletes or scholars composed almost one half of the boys in the leading crowds, the elite social groups; however, they constituted only about 12 percent of the total population of the schools.[87] For girls Coleman noted that personal attractiveness, good personalities, and leadership in activities tended to outweigh academic brilliance as credentials for entry into the elite groups.[88]

Two or three conclusions reached by Coleman are of very great significance to educators. He found that the elites of the student culture were less adult-oriented than the rest of the study body.[89] They appeared to be able to tolerate more parental disapproval than could students who were not members of the elite groups.[90] Second, the elites were less likely than other students to accept the teachers' authority and direction in school activities.[91] He noted that there is a tendency for students who are members of the middle social classes to dominate and control the student youth culture; however, this is modified by the socioeconomic status of the students who compose a majority of the student body.[92] In short, Coleman suggests that "The leading crowd of a school, and thus the norms which that crowd sets, is more than merely a reflection of the student body, with extra middle-class students thrown in. The leading crowd tends to accentuate those very background characteristics already dominant, whether they be upper- or lower-class."[93] That is, the school student culture is apt to be ruled by an elite who represent in the extreme the dominant population group composing the student body.[94] Such findings have enormous implications for policies of school cross-bussing, school ethnic integration, and student involvement in school decision-making processes.

CHAPTER 5

Concepts of Personality and Sociology of Education

Psychology and Sociology of Education

At the outset of the present work, the writers suggested that many concepts with which the teacher of sociology of education will likely deal are of a macroscopic type and universalistic in nature. Such concepts are often used by anthropologists as well as sociologists of education. These include theories of culture, values, mores, sanctions, etc. In this concluding chapter it appears essential to examine the more microscopic concepts that are dealt with by psychologists and the relationship of such concepts to sociology of education. Alex Inkeles has suggested that it is necessary for sociologists in general to possess a working knowledge of psychology. "The thesis . . . is that adequate sociological analysis of many problems is either impossible or severely limited unless we make explicit use of psychological theory and data in conjunction with sociological theory and data. Indeed, I would assert that very little sociological analysis is ever done without using at least an implicit psychological theory."[1]

Numerous psychological theories may be employed by sociologists of education. Psychoanalytic theories tend to view the childhood associations as pivotal in personality formation and learning behavior. Some psychological theories support stimulus-response patterns as the most effective means of accounting for and conditioning attitudes and behavior. Organismic theories attribute great importance to biological factors such as age, intelligence, sex, etc. However, sociologists, in general, are more inclined to place heavy reliance upon theories associated with group organization and process as chief influences in individual personality formation and learning ability.

Irrespective of the theoretical framework employed by sociologists of education, it appears incumbent upon them to attempt in some manner to relate educational structure and process to the more individualized concepts of learning and personality formation. Psychology and educational psychology present the sociologist of education with an opportunity to gain closure and offer a more nearly unified set of concepts and theories. This chapter examines the interrelationship of personality to educational structure and process for specific groups of educators and students. While dozens of other psychological factors and their relationship to education might have been examined, it was felt that personality theory is fundamental to psychology and therefore more potentially worthy of examination than other possible concepts. Inkeles has suggested that "the student of social structure [education in our case] seeks to explain the action consequences of a particular set of institutional arrangements. In order to do this, he must correctly estimate the meaning of these arrangements or their effect on human personality. All institutional arrangements are ultimately mediated through individual human action. The consequences of any institutional arrangement, therefore, depend, at least in part, upon its effect on the human personality, broadly conceived."[2] Bressler indicates that "The ultimate agents of social behavior are individual men acting alone or in concert. Accordingly every theory of society is also implicitly a theory of personality."[3] Let us, therefore, turn to an examination of the impact and relationship of personality development and education upon a select group of students and educators.

The Impact of the Collegiate Experience upon Personality

The research findings generally tend to indicate that formalized learning processes have relatively little effect upon student personality formation in higher institutions of education. Freedman, writing in the early 1960s, noted that colleges and universities are singularly ineffective in molding or shaping students' personalities.[4] Nevitt Sanford has commented that, while college students do achieve considerable information of a cognitive nature, ". . . there is a remarkable discrepancy between the wide public acceptance of a college education and the paucity of demonstrated knowledge that it does some good."[5] Bressler in 1967 noted that "There is little evidence indicating that the personalities or values of students are significantly altered by their collegiate experiences. There is, 'in general,' change in the direction of greater liberalism and sophistication in political, social, and religious outlook, but the magnitude of the change is slight."[6]

At this juncture, it is wise to examine the empirical data collected in the various studies in order to discover possible reasons for the apparent lack of impact of the college experience upon personality formation of students. Philip Jacob has found that the values "do not vary greatly whether they [the students] have pursued a conventional liberal arts program, an integrated general education curriculum, or one of the strictly professional vocational options."[7] While most research certainly supports the assumption that students do achieve a certain amount of cognitive skills as a result of their attendance in classes and participation in academic disciplines, Hodgkinson suggests that they tend to lose between 50 and 75 percent of the factual information within two years of completion of the work.[8] McKeachie has further noted, as have others, that no significant differences can be demonstrated in learning effectiveness as a result of the use of various teaching methods by faculty members. Thus, while many professors and instructors proclaim the superiority of one method such as discussion, free exchange, formalized lectures, independent study, etc., over all others, there is no body of evidence to confirm these assertions.[9] Researchers studying teaching methods have also discovered that size of classes, types of grouping, etc., do not differentially affect student learning or shape personality to any appreciable degree.[10] Bressler has suggested that evidence of this nature should not shock those who work within the collegiate structure because ". . . the university is, after all, primarily dedicated to the purposes of the mind and invests comparatively little energy in systematic efforts to reconstruct character and values."[11]

Such general findings appear to be in complete conflict with many statements contained in the literature of collegiate experience. Many former students would be hard put to deny that their former teachers and professors had a tremendous effect upon their character and personality. Statements such as the following are not at all unusual. " 'It is pretty generally conceded,' writes William L. Kolb, 'that E. A. Ross was the most dramatic and effective classroom teacher in American sociology.' A counter-claim filed by Harry Elmer Barnes on behalf of Sumner declares that he was 'the most inspiring and popular teacher that either Yale or American social sciences has ever produced.' Even the shy and reticent Charles Horton Cooley has been described as a 'great teacher' of mature students."[12] Frank Lloyd Wright has indicated that his former teacher Louis Henri Sullivan had a profound effect upon him and influenced him in many ways.[13] Many former students of Mark Hopkins have endlessly droned on concerning his influence upon them.[14]

Hodgkinson offers an interesting perspective which may help account for such laudatory statements, on the one hand, and divergent empirical data of behavioral scientists, on the other. He suggests that much of the present research in the area lacks conciseness; there is great need for the refinement of methods, techniques, and concepts.[15] Among the reasons Hodgkinson delineates for difficulty in obtaining accurate measures of effect of collegiate faculty members upon the personality of students is the great diversity among students on campuses. Researchers have failed to take this variability and diversity into account in their studies.[16] Most researchers have tended to consider students in the generic category of "all students." More studies of the effect of faculty upon the personality of students should be conducted on the basis of sub-populations within the student body. Not only do differences in levels of maturity, cultural affluence, etc., exist for students but equally great differences often exist within the structural organization of the university. Thus, the College of Education, the College of Arts and Sciences, the College of Agriculture, and the College of Engineering at any major university may differ greatly in what each expects from its students. The teaching faculties in each subdivision may also differ sufficiently as to confound the achievement of overall results of significance.

If, indeed, the formal educational structure and process have little effect upon shaping and molding students' personalities, some of the following factors may be worthy of consideration:

1. Many college and university students on the undergraduate level are often subjected to instructors who are themselves candidates for the doctoral degree and who are little concerned in their teaching with influencing students to any appreciable degree. These graduate instructors are primarily interested in completing a thesis and regard classroom teaching assignments as some form of "slave labor." Such instructors are not likely to be especially committed to influencing students' thinking and behavior. One of the writers recalls recently talking to students on a number of Midwestern campuses. Several such students had reached the end of their sophomore year and had yet to take a class in which a man or woman of professorial rank actually taught the course. Second, freshmen, sophomores, and often entire undergraduate student bodies are apt to be taught primarily by the newly minted assistant professors who may lack the experience and training essential to influence students' personalities. Those faculty

members with such ability may often be retained by the departmental chairmen and deans for teaching only at the graduate level.

2. The growing tendency of students in many colleges and universities to move off campus and find suitable housing within the larger community undoubtedly tends to eliminate to some extent the potential influence of the academic personnel upon the students' behavior and attitudes. Structurally, a college or university appears less able now than formerly to create a close-knit relationship between students and professors. At most schools, they are now more geographically separated. Copley's Open House on Wednesday Nights or Kittridge's Breakfasts enjoyed by an earlier generation of Harvard undergraduates have long since disappeared. The amount and type of informal contacts possible between students is one open to question and inquiry.

3. The increasing heterogeneity and mobility of most student bodies also adds to the difficulty of any single faculty member's having great influence upon student character and personality. Some students come to the university for only one year. Others complete two years of academic work and transfer to another institution. Still others drop out and go a-roaming for a few years. The tremendous divergence of academic plans and programs of students probably adds to the problem of effectively molding and shaping attitudes and behaviors of substantial numbers of students. It must also be added that racial, ethnic, and political divisions on campuses often act in such a manner as to persuade potentially able professors to opt for the relative safety of the sidelines concerning efforts to influence student thinking and character. In a historical period when student bodies were very homogeneous and where a middle-road philosophic view was held by all but a very few students and faculty members, it was possible for an educator to preach and teach in a manner that might have a decisive effect upon a student's thinking and behavior. Today, the conditions for safely doing so have been drastically diminished.

4. College and university administrations have never been seriously concerned with character building. They have often hoped for a modicum of good behavior on the part of students but have done little to analyze the effectiveness of the collegiate structure and process in producing it. Until quite recently little experimentation was done in attempting to create a proper sociological environment for positively affecting students' personality. Administration has generally tended not to reward the "great teachers" on the faculty with raises, promotions, etc., but has encouraged the faculty to build national reputations for their departments and schools by the production of research and literature or by seeking national office in their academic areas of specialization. Such systems of rewards doubtlessly function to discourage great efforts on the part of individual faculty members to orient their careers toward working directly with students. A recent study conducted by one of the writers at the University of Nebraska Medical College asked second-year medical students the degree to which they received encouragement and help in their plans to attend medical school from

undergraduate professors. Of the 105 students who responded to the questionnaire, only eight indicated that they had received "great personal help." Fourteen noted that they had received some personal help, and 64 indicated that they
had done it almost entirely on their own with no help. An additional six noted
that they had been discouraged in their attempts by undergraduate professors.

Changes in Students by Means of Student Culture

Most writers and researchers suggest that it is the student culture
that is the tool by which personalities are developed, modified, and
changed on the college scene. It appears to be the informal group associations that tend to have the greatest impact upon personality. Virtually
all college students can readily recall having experienced and witnessed
the influence of such groups. The freshman strives desperately to
change, to fit into the group's definition of what is proper and correct
behavior, appearance, and attitude. Some feverishly attempt to match
the requirements necessary for admission into a select Greek fraternity
or sorority. One has but to observe formal sorority rush on any Midwestern or Southern campus to note the intense need on the part of the
girls invited to meet the activities and alumni and to conform to house
standards. The hippie group with headquarters in the campus union
building or at some street intersection appears no less concerned than
the Greeks with shaping their personalities to conform to those of the
"in group." The costume, the language, and the mannerisms are as
imitated in one group as in the other. It appears that students' "outlook
on life" may be influenced to a far greater degree by the student culture
than by faculty members, counselors, or administrators on the college
and university level. Such findings would not be contradictory to those
discovered by James Coleman in his studies of students on the secondary
level.[17]

A review of the research and literature suggests there is not just one
single overall student culture on most campuses, but rather a number of
such cultures or sub-cultures may be found. The personality of the student tends to be influenced to a great degree by the particular culture or
sub-culture with which he most closely associates. Pace and Stern attempted to measure the force of certain sociological and psychological
pressures upon students of the nation's campuses. Using Murray's personality needs theory developed in the 1930s as the basis of their research questionnaire, they hypothesized that actions on the part of the
college student result from the interaction between the "press" of the

situational environment (sociological factors) and the "needs" of the individual student (psychological factors). They attempted to measure more than two dozen types of environmental press on a wide variety of campuses. Their questionnaire was structured to measure (1) press for orderliness, (2) press for play, (3) press for ego achievement, (4) press for affiliation, (5) press for exhibitionism, (6) press for dominance, (7) press for adaptiveness, etc. They theorized that different campuses have different student cultures based upon a combination of sociological and psychological variables. The data from the study suggest that in some schools the press for scholarship is dominant. In other schools the press for friendliness was dominant. The findings indicate that in very large urban universities there was press for reflectiveness, humanism, scienticism, understanding and objectivity; and in small liberal arts institutions the dominant press was for sociability and friendliness.[18] It is not too much to suggest that where a dominant press exists to a substantial degree then students' personalities are likely to be influenced in the direction of that dominant press.

Clark and Trow used a somewhat different approach in analyzing student sub-cultures on American campuses. They theorized that two dimensions, (1) affiliation with the college and (2) involvement with ideas, tend to determine the composition of student sub-cultural groups. From these two orientations they evolved four sub-cultural groups. Table I indicates the nature of these sub-cultures.[19]

According to this theory, a college or university may contain any or all four sub-cultures. They do, however, suggest that one sub-culture is likely to be dominant on any given campus.[20] Kees and McDougall have investigated the validity of this fourfold typology designed by Clark and Trow. They theorized that students belonging to the consumer-vocational sub-culture would express great interest in securing an education as a means of occupational employment and give little attention to either intellectual ideas or to school affiliation. They suggested that the collegiate sub-cultural groups would be little concerned with intellectualism but would stress in their behavior affiliation with the school. They felt the nonconformist sub-culture was oriented toward discovering and using modes of self-expression, search for self, and social causality. Members of this sub-culture would accept intellectual ideas but would reject working with or being part of the establishment. Results of their study indicate that 49.70 percent of the students investigated identified with the collegiate sub-culture; 18.19 per cent chose the academic

TABLE I

STUDENT SUB-CULTURAL GROUPS ON AMERICAN CAMPUSES BASED ON
FINDINGS AND CONCEPTS OF CLARK AND TROW

		Involvement with Ideas		
		+		−
		Academic Student		Collegiate Student
	+	Sub-Culture	+	Sub-Culture
Affiliation with College				
		+		−
		Nonconformist		Consumer-Vocational
	−	Sub-Culture	−	Sub-Culture

sub-culture; 30.48 percent identified with the vocational-consumer sub-culture; and 1.73 percent selected the nonconformist sub-culture.[21] Results of their study also confirmed those of Clark and Trow which indicated that land-grant college campuses were dominated by the collegiate and vocational sub-cultures.[22] Further, they suggest that sub-cultural groups are in evidence at the time the students originally arrive on the campus.[23]

There has been criticism of such typologies as oversimplification of the actual situations; nonetheless, they serve as useful material for exploring, in the classroom, the potential influence of sub-cultural groups upon personality formation on the campus scene. Astin and Holland have projected six possible sub-cultural groups on campuses. These include (1) the realist, (2) the intellectual, (3) the social, (4) the conventional, (5) the enterprising, and (6) the artistic.[24] Henry Dyer has suggested that a scheme of this type will provide knowledge of the "way of life, the pressures, and the types of stimulation and frustrations that students are likely to confront on any campus."[25]

Quoting Freedman and Bell, Hodgkinson suggests that two groups exist on the nation's campuses with relatively different goals and ways of life.[26] They possess relatively different methods of adjusting to the campus environment and may, in a sense, be regarded as sub-cultures. Bell labels one group as "scholars" and the other as "intellectuals." Their personality orientations appear to be relatively different. The scholar type, according to Bell, attempts to further his knowledge and extend the frontiers of the knowledge in a subject area. He deals with knowledge in a conventional manner. He accumulates facts and evidence. To the contrary, the intellectual type begins by more or less searching for his own identity. "The intellectual begins with *his* experience, *his* individual perceptions of the world, *his* privileges and deprivations, and judges the world by these sensibilities."[27] These two prototypes very much resemble the groups included in Clark and Trow's academic sub-culture and nonconformist sub-culture.

Dysfunctional Factors on the Campus

There is increasingly evidenced on many campuses a phenomenon that we may call "cultural shock," which many students experience upon their arrival at institutions of higher education. Not all students are able to balance their personality needs with the sociological demands or press of the institutions or cultural groups. One of the writers recalls talking to Dean Dyer of Wake Forest University on several occasions in which he noted the great number of letters he received from students who wrote that they found themselves unable to "cope" with the academic situation, that they had been in almost a state of academic shock, and that they desired, with permission of the dean's office, to leave school for a period of time in order to try to straighten out the situation for themselves.

Barbara E. Ringwald and others, in a study concerned with conflict in the classroom, suggest that there is an impressive array of emotional and interpersonal problems in the average classroom teaching situation and that such problems have a great impact on the students. "Some could be traced to the teacher — for example, to his uncertainty about his proper role in the class and how best to play it. Others arose from the different pressures exerted on the teacher by students with very different expectations, desires and personality styles."[28] What then does happen to the student who is unable to cope with the sociological "pull" of the institution and the "needs" of his own personality?

Spindler has noted that "It has been my contention that the idea of a subtle disorientation within the individual (though also expressed on the group level) as a result of the impact of the curriculum and the collegiate cultural press helps us to understand the pattern of student behavior.[29] Spindler indicates that as a consequence of the academic "lack of fit" students may tend to display personality problems in their attempts to solve the problem of fitting into the institution and student culture. He spells out the patterns of disorientation as: (1) Passive-Withdrawal type — bored, passive observer, tends to withdraw from active participation in almost all phases of academic life; (2) Reactive Type—retreats to the past glories of high school; (3) Compensatory Type—tends to reject earlier accomplishments and achievements, displays frequent concern with crusades and social causes; (4) Adaptive Type—regards education as merely means to an end, short-circuits educational process wherever possible; and (5) Cultural Revisionist Type— begins to adopt an international view, displays considerable anxiety and discomfort in breaking with his cultural past.[30]

Self-Selection and Other Mediating Factors

A process that mediates to some degree the potential impact of the student culture and academic demands upon the individual's personality appears to be that of the phenomenon of self-selection. Most students, according to this theory, have a tendency to seek admission to those institutions in which their personality type is already exemplified by large numbers of students on the campus. Like seeks like within the youth cultures. The individual apparently attempts to locate the school where his personality needs, his family background, and particular habits and behaviors will be most congruent with those of the majority of members of the student body. Most students do not seek out situations in which incongruence is likely to occur. Hodgkinson indicates that "The self-fulfilling prophecy leads us to assume that, if a student comes to college anticipating that his values will change in important directions, the change will occur more often than not."[31] Apparently, before arrival students are able to anticipate whether they possess the personality, intellectual, and behavioral requirements necessary to remain at such institutions as "Podunk State College," "Brain-Drain University," or "Muscles Institute."

In a study touching upon the self-selection process as a mediating factor in potential academic shock, the writers in the fall of 1970 distributed questionnaires to 43 social fraternity housing units on two large Midwestern campuses. From the 1,400 questionnaires returned, it was discovered that almost 50 percent of the men who joined social fraternities made the decision to do so prior to their own graduation from high school. In analyzing the relative importance of the various factors in getting individuals to join the specific house, it was discovered that the most important reason given was that of personality. While 27 percent of the pledges indicated that liking the personalities of the pledges in the house was their first reason for joining, it is possible to add to this category the 22 percent who felt their personalities best fitted those already in the house, and the 7 percent of the pledges who made the decision based on the fact that they already knew several men in the house who were old friends of theirs.[32] Such findings tend to confirm among fraternity memberships the existence of the collegiate sub-culture hypothesized by Clark and Trow. Further, the study revealed that the pledge felt he had to be able to match the rush chairman's family income, physical appearance, religious background, and academic ability. "Should their income or other socio-economic factor be at great variance with that represented by the rush chairman, they seek to pledge another house."[33]

If, indeed, students are able to be self-selecting and enter institutions that already resemble them to a high degree, the question must be raised as to whether in the future such institutions will not take on a relatively narrow definition or cultural press and tend to supersaturate all who enter with that personality imprint. One may question whether this process has not already occurred at such institutions as Berkeley, Harvard, Columbia, etc. Hodgkinson has asserted that colleges in the self-selecting process may increase the proportion of those students who already fit the image themselves.[34] One may hypothesize that institutions of higher education with dominance for one particular cultural press will experience extremely early dropouts during the course of the school year. Where the cultural press is very obvious and where such press does not "fit" the personality needs of the student nor the expectations he holds with regard to educational sociological structure and process, he will rapidly discover the incongruence and withdraw from the institution.

There appears to be a series of structural and organizational means on campuses to mediate the cultural shock experienced by many students. The religious student centers doubtlessly have this as their major goal. The "house system" on many campuses is frequently instituted with the purpose of giving the young man or woman a home away from home. Deans' offices generally are so constituted as to provide students with avenues through which frustrations can be aired and, on occasion, reduced. Clearly, where a college or university highly publicizes its type of press or variety of press, high school students can more correctly anticipate the degree to which their personalities will "fit" the demands of the institution and student culture.

Personality Type and the Teaching Occupation

For a very long time many writers, and perhaps even the general public, have tended to attribute to the teaching population certain personality characteristics. They have tended to view teachers as being not overly masculine, friendly in public situations but introverted in their private lives, high in achievement needs, inhibited in sexual expression, high on authoritarianism (certainly in the context of the classroom), nonmaterialistic, conformists, etc. The question has arisen among many behavioral scientists concerning whether individuals who enter particular occupations and professions tend to do so because they possess certain personality types that are compatible with the roles performed in these status positions. Robert White and others have attempted to analyze the "fit" of certain individual personalities to occupational positions.[35] Max Weber, one of the leading early sociologists, appears to indicate in his analysis of Protestantism and capitalism that certain personality types produced in northern Europe made the new economic system possible.[36] In short, a large group of people had become extremely materialistic, individualistic, and future oriented, and these values had become internalized as part of their personalities. They could be very good capitalists because they, more than most other population groups, possessed particular and unique personality types. Eric Fromm in his classic *Escape from Freedom* appears to suggest the importance of particular personality types and the difficulty of adjustment of such types when confronted with certain sociological situations.[37] Everett Hughes has pointed out that the relationship between personality and occupation is fairly obvious in the case of certain "professions" in primitive societies.[38] One might suggest that the behavioral scientists investigate this relationship in modern society. For example, one might expect that the position of athletic coach would place great merit and great premium upon need for achievement, endurance, heterosexuality, aggression, change, dominance, exhibition, and relatively low premium on such personality characteristics as deference, abasement, neatness, etc. No one has served as counselor to students without being fully aware that certain status positions may be highly attractive to some individuals and equally repelling to others. It appears quite likely that the status position does attract many whose personality types are congruent with the occupational demands and that once the individual has obtained the status position, his personality is further molded to fit the occupational requirements.

If, indeed, it is possible that particular groups have certain personality types in common that predispose them toward certain types of occupations, what is the relationship between the social structure and the personality? Talcott Parsons suggests that personalities are expressed through value orientations or norms in the society. They become, in a sense, the language of personality.[39] Further, the value orientations or norms tend to be expressed, in part, through the status one holds and roles which he performs in the society.[40] Inkeles notes that the culture, social class, and status-role relationships act upon the individual's personality. Where such demands are compatible and congruent with the personality needs, it is possible to hypothesize a productive situation. However, in instances in which the social demands of the culture, social class, and status-roles are such that the personality needs are not satisfied but remain frustrated, the personality produces reactions "which may generate movements of social change in the original sociocultural system."[41] Most behavioral scientists have tended to view social systems and personality systems as highly interrelated; both play upon the other.

Teacher Personality

What personality characteristics do public schoolteachers possess? Goldman, in 1966, attempted to compare the personality need patterns of elementary and secondary schoolteachers in 62 schools within a single Midwestern state. Through the use of the Edward Personal Preference Schedule (EPPS) he found that elementary and secondary teachers differed significantly in their personality needs in 12 of 15 variables.[42] He suggested that elementary school administrators have relatively different types of teachers than do secondary administrators and possibly fewer problems. Table II indicates the relative strength of personality needs of elementary and secondary teachers in Goldman's study.[43]

Goldman's data suggest that secondary teachers have greater personality needs for independence, autonomy, and aggression. Goldman further discovered that elementary and secondary male teachers exhibit very similar personality needs patterns. He found that male and female differences were consistent with the male-female dichotomy found when EPPS was normed. Men appeared to express slightly greater need for autonomy, dominance, endurance, and heterosexuality and less need for affiliation, intraception, dependence, abasement, and change than females in the sample.[44]

TABLE II

COMPARISON OF MEAN SCORES ATTAINED ON THE EDWARDS PERSONAL PREFERENCE
SCHEDULE FOR ELEMENTARY AND SECONDARY SCHOOL TEACHERS

Personality Factor	Elementary Teachers N = 405	Secondary Teachers N = 252	t	p*
1. Achievement	13.57	15.50	−5.905	.001
2. Deference	14.50	13.56	2.828	.01
3. Order	13.13	12.34	1.966	.05
4. Exhibition	13.49	13.86	−1.180	N.S.
5. Autonomy	12.37	13.39	−3.170	.002
6. Affiliation	17.09	14.75	6.784	.002
7. Intraception	17.19	16.24	2.543	.002
8. Succorance	11.96	10.71	3.363	.002
9. Dominance	14.42	13.09	−7.963	.002
10. Abasement	12.25	15.37	3.356	.002
11. Nurturance	16.11	14.39	4.666	.002
12. Change	16.75	16.27	1.317	N.S.
13. Endurance	14.62	14.80	−0.439	N.S.
14. Heterosexuality	12.18	13.48	−2.698	.01
15. Aggression	10.28	12.14	−5.483	.002

*.05 = 1.960; .01 = 2.576; .002 = 3.090

Gillis, in 1964, using the Stern Activities Index with approximately 700 teacher trainees, found that they differed significantly from the norm group, regular college students, on 18 of 30 personality needs scales. The teacher prospects had a greater need for cognitive organization; however, they expressed less need for intellectual analysis, discussion, objectivity, problem solving, and abstraction than did regular college students. The data suggested that these future teachers tended to have greater dependency needs than did regular college students. They expressed greater need for close, mutually supportive relationships, deference, denial of hostility, and order and attention to detail. In the area of impulse needs, education students expressed weaker needs for aggression and assertion but stronger need for emotional expression, combined with a tendency to reject impulsive behavior. The men displayed stronger intellectual needs, while the women exhibited greater dependency needs.[45]

Leeds tends to confirm some of the above findings. In 1956 Leeds administered the Guilford-Zimmerman Temperamental Survey to 300 public schoolteachers in a large Southern city. He found that the teachers' group was higher than the norm group on restraint, objectivity, friendliness, personal relations, and emotional stability. Teachers were lower than the norm group on ascendance and general activity.[46]

One or two interesting studies on specific dimensions of teacher personality may be included here prior to attempting to summarize and discuss the question of whether teachers do possess an occupational personality type. London and Larsen in a study done in the early 1960s, found that teachers tend to have an extremely narrow range of leisure activities. Teachers in the study did not reveal strong commitment to such activities; nor did they participate in many requiring great skill. The teachers appeared to be passive and uninvolved.[47] LeFevre suggests that elementary teachers are more person-oriented, whereas secondary teachers are more subject-oriented. He concluded that teachers are characterized in their personality needs patterns as being relatively intellectual, unaggressive, and conforming.[48]

Several difficulties arise in attempts to measure teacher personality types. First, most researchers have compared them with norms established for general college students. It may be quite possible that they do differ significantly from college students, but so may most other adult professional groups. Second, many researchers have attempted to analyze teacher personality types in a wholesale manner. More valid conclusions can probably be achieved by dividing the teaching population into sub-groups. From the available evidence, the teaching level appears to relate differentially to personality needs. Elementary and secondary teachers appear to be relatively distinct and unique in personality types. While one may, from the available evidence, tend to characterize teachers as being non-aggressive, friendly, with high needs for structure and order, optimistic, and displaying deference to others, there is a great need for refinement and precision in research in the area. Getzels and Jackson have noted that "from the data presented in the Kuder manual the given norms for otherwise undifferentiated groups of teachers are not very discriminating."[49] Inkeles has indicated that "Sociologists have not been distinguished by either the alacrity or the thoroughness with which they have approached this task. Yet solid evidence is gradually being accumulated which reveals that in the 'real' world particular statuses often attract or recruit preponderantly for one or another personality characteristic."[50] Walberg suggests that "the population and subpopulations must be explicitly defined in terms of control variables and results must be differentially analyzed with respect to the different groups of teachers under investigation and interpreted in the light of explicit, preformulated theory."[51]

Notes

CHAPTER 1

1. Brian J. Ashley, Harry Cohen, and Roy G. Slatter, *An Introduction to Sociology of Education* (Bungay, Suffolk, England: The Chaucer Press, 1971), pp. 9-10; Harvey Lee, *The Status of Educational Sociology in Normal Schools, Teachers' Colleges, Colleges, and Universities* (New York: New York University Book Store, 1928), p. 40; Lloyd A. Cook, "Educational Sociology," in Walter S. Monroe (ed.), *Encyclopedia of Educational Research* (Newark: Macmillan Co., 1950), p. 352; Walter R. Smith, "The Need for Consensus in the Field of Educational Sociology," *Journal of Educational Sociology*, 1 (November 1928), 385.

2. Florian Znaniecki, "The Scientific Function of Sociology of Education,"in D. F. Swift (ed.), *Basic Readings in the Sociology of Education* (London: Routledge & Kegan Paul, 1970), pp. 10-12; Cook, ibid., p. 353.

3. Jean Floud and A. H. Halsey, "The Sociology of Education," *Current Sociology*, 7, no. 3 (1958), 165; L. F. Ward, "Education as the Proximate Means of Progress," *Dynamic Sociology* (New York: Appleton-Century-Crofts, 1924), vol. 2, chap. 14.

4. John Dewey, *The School and Society* (Chicago: University of Chicago Press, 1915).

5. Floud and Halsey, op. cit., pp. 165-67.

6. Emile Durkheim in Paul Fauconnet (ed.), *Moral Education* (New York: Free Press, 1961), pp. 1-14; Robert A. Nisbet, *Emile Durkheim* (Englewood Cliffs, N.J.: Prentice-Hall, 1965), pp. 1-6.

7. Ibid., p. 248.

8. Ibid., pp. 249-51 and pp. 21-22.

9. Francis J. Brown, *Educational Sociology* (New York: Greenwood Press, 1969), p. 47; W. B. Brookover, "Sociology of Education: A Definition," *American Sociological Review*, 14 (June 1949), 407.

10. Ibid., and Floud and Halsey, op. cit.

11. Harvey Lee, *Status of Educational Sociology* (New York: New York University Book Store, 1932), p. 5.

12. E. George Payne, *Principles of Educational Sociology: An Outline* (New York: New York University Book Store, 1928), p. 20; and Brown, op. cit., p. 47.

13. Brookover, op. cit.

14. Karl Mannheim and W. A. C. Stewart, *An Introduction to the Sociology of Education* (London: Routledge & Kegan Paul, 1962); Dennis Wrong (ed.), *Max Weber* (Englewood Cliffs, N.J.: Prentice-Hall, 1970); Floud and Halsey, op. cit., pp. 168-81.

15. Floud and Halsey, op. cit., p. 178.

16. Ibid.

17. Charles Bidwell, "Educational Sociology," in R. Ebel (ed.), *Encyclopedia of Eductional Research* (New York: Macmillan Co., 1969), p. 1244.

18. Floud and Halsy, op. cit., p. 178.

19. Ibid., p. 169.

20. Ibid., p. 166.

21. Wilbur B. Brookover and David Gottlieb, *A Sociology of Education* (New York: American Book Co., 1964), p. 9; Willard Waller, *The Sociology of Teaching* (New York: John Wiley, 1932). pp. 49-67, 195-98.

22. Waller, ibid., pp. 18-19.

23. Brookover, op. cit., p. 408.

24. G. S. Herrington, "The Status of Educational Sociology Today," *Journal of Educational Sociology,* 21 (November 1947), 129.

25. W. B. Brookover, "Sociology of Education: A Definition," op. cit., pp. 407-15.

26. Ibid., p. 408.

27. Ibid., pp. 407-15.

28. Adapted from W. B. Brookover's analysis in "Sociology of Education: A Definition," op. cit.

29. Donald A. Hansen, "The Uncomfortable Relation of Sociology and Education," in *On Education—Sociological Perspective* (New York: John Wiley, 1967), pp. 9-10.

30. Ibid.

31. Lloyd Allen Cook and Elaine F. Cook, *A Sociological Approach to Education* (New York: McGraw-Hill, 1950).

32. W. Warren Kallenbach and Harold M. Hodges, Jr., *Education and Society* (Columbus, Ohio: Charles E. Merrill, 1963).

33. Blaine E. Mercer and Edwin R. Carr, *Education and the Social Order* (New York: Rinehart & Company, 1957).

34. Brown, op. cit., p. 49.

35. Gale Edward Jensen, *Educational Sociology* (New York: The Center for Applied Research in Education, 1965), pp. 1-13.

36. Ibid., p. 6.

37. Ibid., p. 8.

38. W. Taylor, "The Sociology of Education," in J. W. Tibble (ed.), *The Study of Education* (London: Routledge & Kegan Paul, 1967), p. 191; D. F. Swift, *The Sociology of Education: Introductory Analytical Perspectives,* (London: Routledge & Kegan Paul, 1969), p. 4.

39. Hansen, op. cit., pp. 30-33.

40. Brookover and Gottlieb, op. cit., p. 10.

41. Richard G. Hoyme, "Current Status of Educational Sociology," *Journal of Educational Sociology,* 35 (November 1961), 131-32.

42. Ibid.

43. Unpublished study conducted by Keith W. Prichard and Thomas H. Buxton, University of Nebraska, 1972. Five hundred provosts and academic deans were contacted for this information.

44. Hoyme, op. cit., p. 129.

45. Ibid.

46. Eldon E. Snyder, "Sociology of Education: A Description of the Field," *Sociology and Social Research*, 52 (January 1968) 29.

47. Ibid., p. 30.

48. Hoyme, op. cit., p. 129.

49. Herbert Blumer, "What Is Wrong with Social Theory," *American Sociological Review*, 19, no. 1 (February 1954), 7.

50. Ibid.

51. Jerome S. Bruner, Jacqueline J. Goodnow, and George A. Austin, *A Study of Thinking* (New York: John Wiley, 1967), pp. 11-13.

52. Snyder, op. cit.

53. Hoyme, op. cit., pp. 130-31.

54. Bernard N. Meltzer and J. G. Manis, "The Teaching of Sociology," *Teaching of the Social Sciences in the United States* (Paris: UNESCO, 1968), p. 94.

CHAPTER 2

1. Clyde Kluckhohn, *Culture and Behavior* (Glencoe, Ill.: Free Press, 1962), pp. 71-73; Ritchie P. Lowry and Robert P. Rankin, *Sociology: Social Science and Social Conscience* (New York: Charles Scribner's Sons, 1972), p. 105.

2. Theodore Brameld, *Cultural Foundations of Education* (New York: Harper & Brothers, 1957), pp. 5-7; W. B. Brookover and Edsel L. Erickson, *Society, Schools, and Learning* (Boston: Allyn & Bacon, 1965), pp. 20-23.

3. Kimball Young and Raymond W. Mack, *Systematic Sociology* (New York: American Book Co., 1962), p. 39.

4. S. M. Miller and Frank Riessmann, *Social Class and Social Policy* (New York: Basic Books, 1968), pp. 52-53, 64; James S. Coleman, "Equal Schools or Equal Students?" *Public Interest*, 4 (Summer 1966), 70-75.

5. Ralph Linton, *The Study of Man* (New York: Appleton-Century, 1936), pp. 282-84.

6. Ibid.

7. Ibid.

8. Ibid.

9. Ibid.

10. Ibid.

11. Ibid.

12. Lloyd Allen Cook and Elaine Forsyth Cook, *A Sociological Approach to Education* (New York: McGraw-Hill, 1950), pp. 6-7.

13. Robert C. Angell, *The Integration of American Society* (New York: McGraw-Hill, 1941), p. 215.

14. Harold Hodgkinson, *Education in Social and Cultural Perspective* (Englewood Cliffs. N.J.: Prentice-Hall, 1962), p. 12.

15. Florence Kluckhohn, "Variations in the Basic Values of Family Systems," in D. F. Swift (ed.), *Basic Readings in the Sociology of Education* (London: Routledge & Kegan Paul, 1970), pp. 199-216.

16. Alex Inkeles and Daniel J. Levinson, "National Character: The Study of Modal Personality and Sociocultural Systems," in Gardner Lindzey and Elliot Aronson (eds.), *The Handbook of Social Psychology*, (Reading, Mass.: Addison-Wesley, 1969), pp. 435-36.

17. Florence Kluckhohn, "Dominant and Substitute Profiles of Cultural Orientation: Their Significance for the Analysis of Social Stratification," *Social Forces,* 28 (1950), 376-93.

18. Florence Kluckhohn, "Some Reflections on the Nature of Cultural Integration and Change," in Edward A. Tiryakian (ed.), *Sociological Theory, Values, and Sociocultural Change* (London: Free Press of Glencoe, 1962), pp. 212-45.

19. George D. Spindler, "Current Anthropology," in George D. Spindler (ed.), *Education and Culture* (New York: Holt, Rinehart & Winston, 1963), pp. 20-23.

20. Talcott Parsons, *The Social System* (Glencoe, Ill.: Free Press, 1951), pp. 101-12.

21. Ibid., p. 105.

22. Talcott Parsons, *Sociological Theory and Modern Society* (New York: Free Press, 1967), pp. 192-219.

23. Parsons, *The Social System,* pp. 105-06.

24. Talcott Parsons and Winston White, "The Link Between Character and Society," in Talcott Parsons (ed.), *Social Structure and Personality* (London: Free Press of Glencoe, 1964), pp. 183-235.

25. Ibid., pp. 202-05; also Spindler, op. cit., pp. 40-41.

26. Ibid.

27. Ibid., pp. 136-37. Spindler suggests that his value system is based to a large degree upon the system devised by David Riesman, who views the relationship between society and individual personality as being linked by three mechanisms, each one of which indicative of a source of direction—tradition, inner, and other. Riesman feels that these value orientation patterns or typologies are universal, inasmuch as no society or person is wholly dependent upon one but rather tends to be dominated by one. Hence, principal reliance is placed upon one.

28. Ibid.

29. Ibid., p. 139.

30. Ibid.

31. Ibid., pp. 142-43.

32. Ibid., p. 145.

33. Florence Kluckhohn and F. Strodtbeck, *Variations in Value Orientation* (Evanston, Ill.: Row, Peterson, 1961), pp. 10-20.

34. Florence Kluckhohn, "Some Reflections on the Nature of Cultural Integration and Change," op. cit., pp. 222, 230, 231.

35. Joseph P. Lash, *Eleanor and Franklin* (New York: Norton Press, 1971).

36. Pearl Buck, *The Good Earth* (New York: John Day, 1931).

37. George Orwell, *Nineteen Eighty-Four* (New York: Harcourt, Brace & World, 1949).

38. Florence Kluckhohn, "Some Reflections of the Nature of Cultural Integration and Change," op. cit.

39. Ibid.

40. Ibid.

41. Boris Leonidovich Pasternak, *Doctor Zhivago* (New York: Pantheon Books, 1958).

42. Florence Kluckhohn, "Some Reflections on the Nature of Cultural Integration and Change," op. cit.

43. Ibid.

44. Ibid.

45. Ibid.

46. Ibid.
47. Ibid.
48. Jean Jacques Rousseau, *Emile* (Boston: Heath's Pedagogical Library, 1909).
49. Florence Kluckhohn, "Some Reflections on the Nature of Cultural Integration and Change," op. cit.; also see Julian Freund, *The Sociology of Max Weber* (New York: Pantheon Books, 1968), p. 205 for description of Protestant ethic, etc.
50. Spindler, op. cit., pp. 136-37.
51. Ibid., p. 132.
52. Ibid.
53. Ibid.
54. Ibid., pp. 139-41.
55. Ibid., pp. 133-35.
56. Ibid.
57. Ibid., p. 138.
58. Ibid., p. 139.
59. Ibid., p. 138.
60. Ibid.
61. Ibid., pp. 136-37.
62. Ibid., p. 136.
63. Max Weber, *The Protestant Ethic and the Spirit of Capitalism* (New York: Oxford University Press, 1958); see also Freund, op. cit., pp. 203-309.
64. Spindler, op. cit.
65. Ibid.
66. James S. Coleman, *The Adolescent Society* (New York: Free Press, 1961); James S. Coleman, "Academic Achievement and the Structure of Competition," *Harvard Educational Review*, 29 (Fall 1959), 303-51.
67. Spindler, op. cit., p. 137.
68. Ibid., p. 139.
69. Ibid., p. 137.
70. Ibid.
71. Ibid., p. 143.
72. W. F. Ogburn, *Social Change with Respect to Culture and Original Nature* (New York: Viking Press, 1922), pp. 200-01.
73. Harold L. Hodgkinson, *Education, Integration, and Social Change* (Englewood Cliffs, N.J.: Prentice-Hall, 1967), pp. 202-03.

CHAPTER 3

1. Harold W. Pfautz, "The Current Literature on Social Stratification: A Critique and Bibliography," *American Journal of Sociology* 58 (January 1953), 391-418.
2. Lloyd Warner, *Yankee City Series* (New Haven: Yale University Press, 1963); A. Davis and B. Gardner, *Deep South* (Chicago: University of Chicago Press, 1941); August Hollingshead, *Elmtown's Youth* (New York: John Wiley, 1949); Robert J. Havighurst, "Social Class and Personality Structure," *Sociology and Social Research*, 36 (July-August 1952), 355-63.
3. Bernard Barber, Social Stratification (New York: Harcourt, Brace, 1957); Reinhard Bendix and S. Lipset (eds.), *Class, Status and Power* (Glencoe, Ill.: Free Press, 1953); Gerhard E. Lenski, "Social Stratification," in Joseph S. Roucek (ed.), *Contemporary*

Sociology (New York: Philosophical Library, 1958); Harold Pfautz, op. cit., 58 (January, 1953), 391-418; D. G. MacRae, "Social Stratification: A Trend Report and Bibliography," *Current Sociology*, 1 (1953-54), 7-31; C. W. Mills, *The Power Elite* (New York: Oxford University Press, 1956); P. Hatt, "Occupations and Social Stratification," *American Journal of Sociology*, 55 (May 1950), 533-43; N. Rogoff, *Recent Trends in Occupational Mobility* (New York: Free Press, 1953).

4. Lenski, Ibid., pp. 526-27.

5. Albert J. Reiss, Jr., "Some Sociological Issues About American Communities," in Talcott Parsons (ed.), *American Sociology* (New York: Basic Books, 1968), pp. 66-67.

6. Bernard Barber, "Social Stratification Structure and Trends of Social Mobility in Western Society," in *American Sociology*, ibid., pp. 184-95.

7. Karl Marx, "The Class Struggle," in Gloria B. Levitas (ed.), *Culture and Consciousness* (New York: George Braziller, 1967), pp. 76-85; Herbert Aptheker, *Marxism and Alienation* (New York: Humanities Press, 1965), pp. 15-25.

8. Donald MacRae, *Ideology and Society* (New York: Free Press, 1962), pp. 65-68.

9. Paul F. Lazarsfeld, "Measurement," in Talcott Parsons (ed.), *American Sociology*, op. cit., pp. 98-103.

10. Vance Packard, *The Status Seekers* (New York: David McKay, 1959).

11. Robert Perrucci, "Education, Stratification, and Mobility," in Donald A. Hansen and Joel E. Gerstl (eds.), *On Education — Sociological Perspectives* (New York: John Wiley, 1967), pp. 107-08.

12. Ibid., pp. 108-09.

13. W. Lloyd Warner, Robert J. Havighurst, and Martin B. Loeb, *Who Shall Be Educated?* (New York: Harper, 1944), p. xi.

14. Perrucci, op. cit., pp. 105-08.

15. Ibid., pp. 109-10.

16. Ibid.

17. Marvin Bressler, "Sociology and Collegiate General Education," in Paul F. Lazarsfeld et al. (eds.), *The Uses of Sociology* (New York: Basic Books, 1967), p. 47.

18. Harold L. Wilensky and Hugh Edwards, "The Skidders: Ideological Adjustments of Downward Mobile Workers," *American Sociological Review*, 24 (April 1959), 215-31.

19. Packard, op. cit., pp. 253-63.

20. W. Lloyd Warner, M. Meeker, and Kenneth Eells, *Social Class in America: A Manual for Procedure for Measure of Social Status* (Chicago: Science Research Associates, 1949); Richard Centers, *The Psychology of Social Classes* (Princeton: Princeton University Press, 1949).

21. Among those presenting critical views of the generally accepted methods of measuring social stratification are the following: Gerhard E. Lenski, "Status Crystallization: A Non-Vertical Dimension of Social Status," *American Sociological Review*, 19 (August 1954), 405-13; Harold W. Pfautz and Otis D. Duncan, "A Critical Evaluation of Warner's Work in Community Stratification," *American Sociological Review*, 15 (April 1950), 202-15; Ruth R. Kornhauser, "The Warner Approach to Social Stratification," in Richard Bendix and Seymour M. Lipset (eds.), *Class, Status and Power* (Glencoe, Ill.: Free Press, 1953).

22. W. Lloyd Warner and Paul S. Lunt, *The Status Systems of a Modern Community* (New Haven: Yale University Press, 1942), chap. 1.

23. W. Lloyd Warner, Marcia Meeker, and Kenneth Eells, *Social Class in America* (Chicago: Science Research Associates, 1949), chap. 2 and p. 43.

24. Ibid.

25. Ibid. and Kimball Young and Raymond Mack, *Systematic Sociology* (New York: American Book Co., 1962), pp. 180-81.

26. Young and Mack, ibid.

27. E. Digby Baltzell, *The Protestant Establishment: Aristocracy and Caste in America* (New York: Random House, 1964), pp. 80-86.

28. John P. Marquand, *The Late George Apley* (New York: Grosset & Dunlap, 1936).

29. Joseph P. Lash, *Eleanor and Franklin* (New York: Norton Press, 1971).

30. Thorstein Veblen, *The Theory of the Leisure Class* (New York: Macmillan Co., 1899).

31. C. Wright Mills, *The Power Elite* (New York: Oxford University Press, 1956); Adolph A. Berle, *Power Without Property* (New York: Harcourt, Brace, 1959).

32. Bressler, op. cit., pp. 46-48.

33. "The People of the United States—A Self-Portrait," *Fortune* (February 1940), pp. 14-20.

34. Centers, op. cit., p. 27.

35. Ibid.

36. Ibid.

37. Ibid. Also Ivan D. Steiner, "Some Social Values Associated with Objectively Defined Social Class Membership," *Social Forces*, 31 (May 1953), 327-32.

39. Centers, ibid.

39. Ibid.

40. John C. Leggett, "Working-Class Consciousness, Race, and Political Choice," *American Journal of Sociology*, 69 (September 1963), 171-76.

41. Herbert Luethy, "Over Again: Calvinism and Capitalism," in Dennis Wrong (ed.), *Max Weber* (Englewood Cliffs, N.J.: Prentice-Hall, 1970), pp. 123-34; Young and Macks, op. cit., p. 215; Pitirim A. Sorokin, *Social and Cultural Mobility* (Glencoe, Ill.: Free Press, 1959), pp. 533-36.

42. Gerhard E. Lenski, "Social Stratification," op. cit., pp. 523-25.

43. Ibid.

44. Young and Macks, op. cit., p. 217.

45. J. O. Hertzler, "Some Tendencies Toward a Closed System in the United States," *Social Forces*, 30 (May 1952), 313-23.

46. Centers, op. cit., p. 180.

47. Francis E. Merrill, *Sociology and Culture* (Englewood Cliffs, N.J.: Prentice-Hall, 1965), p. 335.

48. Ibid.; C. F. Westoff, "Differential Fertility in the United States," *American Sociological Review*, 19 (October 1954), 549-61.

49. Young and Mack, op. cit., pp. 214-15.

CHAPTER 4

1. Kingsley Davis, "Status and Related Concepts," in Bruce J. Biddle and Edwin J. Thomas (eds.), *Role Theory* (New York: John Wiley, 1966), p. 67.

2. Kimball Young and Raymond W. Mack, *Systematic Sociology* (New York: American Book Co., 1962), p. 139.

3. Earl H. Bell and John Sirjamaki, *Social Foundations of Human Behavior* (New York: Harper & Row, 1965), pp. 439-42.

4. Ibid.

5. Bruce J. Biddle and Edwin J. Thomas, *Role Theory* (New York: John Wiley, 1966), p. 7.

6. Ronald G. Corwin, *A Sociology of Education* (New York: Appleton-Century-Crofts, 1965), pp. 64-65.

7. Marion J. Levy, Jr., *The Structure of Society* (Princeton: Princeton University Press, 1952), p. 160.

8. Francis E. Merrill, *Sociology and Culture* (Englewood Cliffs, N.J.: Prentice-Hall, 1965), p. 304.

9. Robert K. Merton, *Social Theory and Social Structure* (New York: Free Press, 1968), pp. 123-24.

10. Young and Mack, op. cit., p. 140; also Davis, op. cit., p. 68.

11. Davis, ibid.

12. Oscar A. Oeser and Frank Harary, "Role Structure: A Description in Terms of Graph Theory," in Biddle and Thomas (eds.), *Role Theory,* op. cit., pp. 93-94.

13. Merrill, op. cit., p. 177.

14. Talcott Parsons, *The Social System* (Glencoe, Ill.: Free Press, 1951), pp. 25-28.

15. Roscoe C. Hinkle, Jr., and Alvin Boskoff, "*Social Stratification in Perspective,*" in Howard Becker and Alvin Boskoff (eds.), *Modern Sociological Theory* (New York: Dryden Press, 1957), p. 387.

16. Hugh D. Duncan, "Sociology in Art, Literature and Music: Social Contexts of Symbolic Experience," in Becker and Boskoff (eds.), ibid., pp. 488-97.

17. Harold L. Hodgkinson, *Education, Interaction and Social Change* (Englewood Cliffs, N.J.: Prentice-Hall, 1967), p. 13.

18. Levy, op. cit., p. 162.

19. Clarence C. Schrag, Otto N. Larsen, and William R. Catton, Jr., *Sociology* (New York: Harper & Row, 1968), pp. 161-65; also Becker and Boskoff, op. cit., p. 291.

20. Grace Metalious, *Peyton Place* (New York: Simon & Schuster, 1956).

21. Neal Gross, Alexander W. McEachern, and Ward S. Mason, "Role Conflict and Its Resolution," in Biddle and Thomas (eds.), *Role Theory,* op. cit., pp. 287-88.

22. Robert K. Merton, "Research and Sociological Theory," in Peter I. Rose (ed.), *The Study of Society* (New York: Random House, 1967), pp. 46-47.

23. Merrill, op. cit., p. 179.

24. Merton, *Social Theory and Social Structure,* op. cit., p. 422.

25. Charles P. Loomis and Zona K. Loomis, "Robert K. Merton as a Structural Analyst," in Charles P. Loomis and Zona K. Loomis (eds.), *Modern Social Theories* (Princeton: D. Van Nostrand, 1961), pp. 281-82; Edwin J. Thomas and Bruce J. Biddle, op. cit., pp. 40-41.

26. Kimball Young and Linton Freeman, "Social Psychology and Sociology," in *Modern Sociological Theory,* op. cit., pp. 464-65.

27. Keith W. Prichard and Thomas H. Buxton, *Role Model Identity in Classroom Teaching of 142 "Teachers of the Year,"* Monograph, *College Student Journal* (Milwaukee: Project Education, September-October, 1972), pp. 1-10.

28. Ibid., p. 3.

29. Abraham Zaleznek and Ann Jardim, "Management," in Paul F. Lazarsfeld, William H. Sewell, and Harold L. Wilensky (eds.), *Uses of Sociology* (New York: Basic Books, 1967), p. 211.

30. Arnold M. Rose, *Sociology* (New York: Knopf, 1965), p. 291; and Davis, op. cit., pp. 69-74.

31. Earl H. Bell and John Sirjamaki, *Social Foundations of Human Behavior* (New York: Harper & Row, 1965), p. 198.

32. Davis, op. cit., pp. 69-73.

33. Ibid.

34. Merton, "Instability and Articulation in the Role-Set," in Biddle and Thomas (eds.), *Role Theory*, op. cit., p. 282; also Merton, *Social Theory and Social Structure*, op. cit., pp. 41-45.

35. Ibid., p. 42.

36. Robert O. Blood and Donald M. Wolfe, "Division of Labor in American Families," in Bruce J. Biddle and Edwin J. Thomas (eds.), *Role Theory*, op. cit., p. 266.

37. Brian J. Ashley, Harry Cohen, and Roy G. Slatter, *An Introduction to the Sociology of Education* (London: Macmillan and Co., 1971), pp. 23-24.

38. K. Yamamoto and H. F. Dizney, "Eight Professors — A Study on College Students' Preferences Among Their Teachers," *Journal of Educational Psychology*, 57 (June 1966), 146.

39. Robert H. Knapp, "Changing Functions of the College Professor," in Nevitt Sanford (ed.), *The American College* (New York: John Wiley, 1962), pp. 291-92.

40. Ibid.

41. Charles H. Monson, Jr., "Professor's Four Faces," *A.A.U.P. Bulletin*, 53 (March 1967), 11-14.

42. John W. Gustad, "The Complete Academician," *The Record*, 65 (November 1963), 112-22.

43. Biddle and Thomas, op. cit., pp. 34-35.

44. Burton R. Clarke, "Faculty Culture," in Terry F. Lunsford (ed.), The Study of Campus Cultures (Berkeley: Center for Study of Higher Education, 1963), pp. 52-53.

45. Eric Hoyle, *The Role of the Teacher* (London: Routledge & Kegan Paul, 1969), pp. 52-53.

46. Alvin Gouldner, "Red Tape as a Problem," in Robert Merton (ed.), *Reader in Bureaucracy* (Glencoe, Ill.: Free Press, 1952), pp. 410-18.

47. Merton, *Social Theory and Social Structure*, op. cit., pp. 251-54.

48. Ibid., p. 253.

49. Robert C. Stone, "The Sociology of Bureaucracy," in Joseph S. Roucek (ed.), *Contemporary Sociology* (New York: Philosophical Library, 1958), pp. 432-433.

50. Merton, *Social Theory and Social Structure*, op. cit., p. 250.

51. Harry L. Miller and Roger R. Woock, *Social Foundations of Education* (Hinsdale, Ill.: Dryden Press, 1970), p. 301.

52. Ibid.

53. Ritchie P. Lowry and Robert P. Rankin, *Sociology* (New York: Charles Scribner's Sons, 1972), p. 323; also Neal Gross and Joshua A. Fishman, "The Management of Educational Establishments," in Paul Lazarsfeld, W. Sewell, and H. Wilensky (eds.), *The Uses of Sociology* (New York: Basic Books, 1967), p. 314.

54. Miller and Woock, op. cit., p. 301.

55. Bernard Barber, "Is American Business Becoming Professionalized?" in Edward A. Tiryakian (ed.), *Sociological Theory, Values and Sociocultural Change* (London: Collier-Macmillan, 1963), p. 139.

56. Miller and Woock, op. cit., p. 306.

57. Ibid.

58. Neal Gross and Robert E. Herriott, *Staff Leadership in Public Schools* (New York: John Wiley, 1965), p. 151.

59. Ibid., p. 153.

60. Ibid., p. 157.

61. Merrill, op. cit., p. 391.

62. Ibid.

63. Ibid., pp. 391-92.

64. Miller and Woock, op. cit., pp. 308-09.

65. August B. Hollingshead, *Elmtown's Youth* (New York: John Wiley, 1949).

66. C. Wayne Gordon, *The Social System of the High School* (Glencoe, Ill.: Free Press, 1957).

67. James S. Coleman, *The Adolescent Society* (New York: Free Press, 1961).

68. Burton R. Clark, *Educating the Expert Society* (San Francisco: Chandler, 1962).

69. Talcott Parsons, "Youth in the Context of American Society," *Daedalus*, 91 (Winter 1962) 97-123.

70. Hollingshead, op. cit., pp. 149, 161-203.

71. Ibid., p. 441.

72. Ibid., p. 168.

73. Ibid.

74. Ibid., pp. 185-92.

75. Ibid., p. 172.

76. Clark, op. cit., pp. 244-70.

77. Coleman, op. cit., p. 5.

78. Ibid., p. 4.

79. Sarane Boocock, *An Introduction to the Sociology of Learning* (Boston: Houghton-Mifflin, 1972). pp. 210-11.

80. Ibid., p. 210.

81. Coleman, op. cit., p. 3.

82. Clark, op. cit., pp. 245-70.

83. Ibid., pp. 254-57.

84. Ibid., pp. 263-69.

85. Coleman, op. cit., pp. 5-6, 141, 285-87.

86. Ibid., p. ix.

87. Ibid., p. 148-49.

88. Ibid., pp. 30, 164-65.

89. Ibid., pp. 140-41 and p. 6.

90. Ibid., pp. 140-42 and p. 6.

91. Ibid.

92. Ibid., p. 109.

93. Ibid.

94. Ibid.

CHAPTER 5

1. Alex Inkeles, "Personality and Social Structure," in Talcott Parsons (ed.), *American Sociology* (New York: Basic Books, 1968), p. 3.

2. Ibid.

3. Marvin Bressler, "Sociology and Collegiate General Education," in Paul F. Lazarsfeld, William H. Sewell, and Harold L. Wilensky (eds.), *The Uses of Sociology* (New York: Basic Books, 1967), p. 58.

4. Mervin B. Freedman and Winslow R. Hatch, *Impact of College* (Washington, D.C.: U.S. Department of Health, Education, and Welfare, O.E.–50011, No. 4), pp. 16-17.

5. Nevitt Sanford, *The American College* (New York: John Wiley, 1962), p. 805.

6. Bressler, op. cit., p. 52.

7. Philip E. Jacob, *Changing Values in College* (New York: Harper, 1957), p. 5; David Riesman, "The Jacob Report," *American Sociological Review*, 23 (December 1958), 732-38. Jacob suggests a few colleges do have the "peculiar potency" to produce change in students' values and attitudes.

8. Harold L. Hodgkinson, *Education, Interaction, and Social Change* (Englewood Cliffs, N.J.: Prentice-Hall, 1967), p. 187.

9. W. J. McKeachie, "Research on Teaching at the College and University Level," in N. L. Gage (ed.), *Handbook of Research on Teaching* (Chicago: Rand McNally, 1963), pp. 1126-72.

10. Ibid.

11. Bressler, op. cit., p. 53.

12. Nathan Glazer, "The Ideological Uses of Sociology," in Paul F. Lazarsfeld, William H. Sewell, and Harold L. Wilensky (eds.), *The Uses of Sociology* (New York: Basic Books, 1967), p. 64.

13. Houston Peterson, *Great Teachers* (New York: Vintage Books, 1946), p. 53.

14. Ibid., p. 76.

15. Hodgkinson, op. cit., p. 186.

16. Ibid.

17. James S. Coleman, *The Adolescent Society* (New York: Free Press, 1961).

18. C. Robert Pace and George G. Stern, "An Approach to the Measurement of Psychological Characteristics of College Environments," *Journal of Educational Psychology*, 49 (October 1958), 269-77.

19. Burton R. Clark and Martin Trow, "Organizational Context," in *College Peer Groups* (Chicago: Aldine Publishing Co., 1966); Henry S. Dyer, "Admissions-College and University," in Robert L. Ebel (ed.), *Encyclopedia of Educational Research* (London: Macmillan Co., 1969), p. 34; Burton R. Clark, *Educating the Expert Society* (San Francisco: Chandler, 1962), p. 210.

20. Dyer, ibid., p. 34.

21. Donald J. Kees and William P. McDougall, "A Validation Study of the Clark-Trow College Subculture Typology," *The Journal of College Student Personnel*, 12 (May 1971), 193-94.

22. Ibid., p. 194.

23. Ibid.

24. Alexander W. Astin, "Further Validation of the Environmental Assessment Technique," *Journal of Educational Psychology*, 54 (August 1963), 217-26, Alexander W. Astin, "Distribution of Students Among Higher Educational Institutions," *Journal of Educational Psychology*, 55 (October 1964), 277.

25. Dyer, op. cit., p. 34.

26. Hodgkinson, op. cit., pp. 182-83.

27. Ibid.

28. Barbara E. Ringwald, Richard D. Mann, Robert Rosenwein, and Wilbert J. Mc-Keachie, "Conflict and Style in the College Classroom—An Intimate Study," *Psychology Today*, 4 (February 1971), 45.

29. George D. Spindler, *Education and Culture* (New York: Holt, Rinehart, & Winston, 1963), p. 264.

30. Ibid., pp. 263-64.

31. Hodgkinson, op. cit., p. 189.

32. Keith W. Prichard and Thomas H. Buxton, "The Social Fraternity System: Its Increasing Problems," *Journal of College Personnel*, 13 (May 1972), 221-22.

33. Ibid.

34. Hodgkinson, op. cit., pp. 188-89.

35. Robert W. White, *Lives in Progress* (New York: Holt, Rinehart, & Winston, 1962).

36. Alex Inkeles, "Personality and Social Structure," in Robert K. Merton, Leonard Broom, and Leonard S. Cottrell, Jr. (eds.), *Sociology Today* (New York: Basic Books, 1959), p. 256.

37. Ibid., pp. 255-56.

38. Alex Inkeles and Daniel J. Levinson, "National Character: The Study of Modal Personality and Sociocultural Systems," *The Handbook of Social Psychology*, vol. 4 (Reading, Mass.: Addison-Wesley, 1969), p. 474.

39. Charles Loomis and Zona K. Loomis, "Talcott Parson's Social Theory," in Charles Loomis and Zona K. Loomis (eds.), *Modern Social Theories* (Princeton: D. Van Nostrand, 1961), pp. 333.

40. Ibid.

41. Inkeles, *Sociology Today*, op. cit., p. 261.

42. Harvey Goldman, "Differential Needs Patterns: Implications for Principals," *The School Review*, 77 (September-December 1969), 268.

43. Ibid.

44. Ibid., p. 273.

45. John Gillis, "Personality Needs of Future Teachers," *Educational Psychology and Measurement*, 24 (Fall 1964), 589-600.

46. J. W. Getzels and P. W. Jackson, "The Teacher's Personality and Characteristics," in N. L. Gage (ed.), *Handbook of Research on Teaching* (Chicago: Rand McNally, 1963), p. 548.

47. Perry London and Donald E. Larsen, "Teachers' Leisure," *Teachers' College Record*, 65 (March 1964), 544-45.

48. Carol LeFevre, "Teacher Characteristics and Careers," *Review of Educational Research*, 37 (October 1967), 437.

49. Herbert J. Walberg, "The Development of Teacher Personality Multivariate Theory and Analysis," *School Review*, 75 (Summer 1967), 188.

50. Alex Inkeles, "Personality and Social Structure," in *Sociology Today*, op. cit., p. 264.

51. Walberg, op. cit., p. 195.